Successful
Late
Bloomers

Second Edition

Successful Late Bloomers

Second Edition

The story of late-in-life achievement: the people,
strategies and research

By J.M. Orend

ISBN: 978-0-9952842-0-3

Copyright

Publisher

Lomic Books
Kitchener, Ontario
www.lomicbooks.com

For my dad,

Vaclav Lomic

Aging is not lost youth,
but a new stage of
opportunity and strength.

— Betty Friedan

Table of Contents

Section Four
Getting Started: Now What?

Section Five
Inspirational Late-bloomer Lists

Section Six
The Rest

Introduction

"There is nothing in a caterpillar that tells you it's going to be a butterfly."

— R. Buckminster Fuller

Successful Late Bloomers takes a look at how late bloomers achieve their late-in-life success using real life stories, scientific research, and simple insights.

You will learn about many successful artists, entrepreneurs, and athletes whose most extraordinary achievements happened after they turned forty.

In fact, in *Successful Late Bloomers* you will read about people who didn't even start their most important work until they were seventy, eighty, or even ninety years old.

Hopefully, you will be inspired as you learn about

each type of late bloomer — *Bad News*, *Messy*, and *New Stage*; and the many different people who found late-in-life success in their own way.

Despite conventional wisdom, late bloomers can derive many advantages from their age. How aging contributes to success is highlighted in chapters four to six.

In the next section, the common components of late-blooming success are discussed. Learn about the effective strategies that late bloomers apply to achieve their goals. These strategies are followed by the section, "Getting Started: Now What?" which takes a look at different approaches to the hardest part of the late-blooming journey — getting started.

The final part of *Successful Late Bloomers* is all about inspiration. There are several late-bloomer lists, which are meant to serve as an important reminder that late-blooming success is achievable.

I hope that this book will be useful to every reader in two ways. First, it demonstrates that success later in life is a common experience; and second, it features some of the helpful approaches used by successful late bloomers.

If I did my job well, and I certainly hope I did, by the end of this book, you will see the second half of life as rich with possibilities as the first, perhaps even more.

Section One

. . .

Types
of
Late
Bloomers

Chapter I
Messy Late
Bloomers

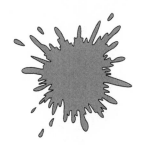

*"People take the longest possible paths,
digress to numerous dead ends, and make
all kinds of mistakes. Then historians
come along and write summaries of this
messy, nonlinear process and make it
appear like a simple, straight line."*

— Dean Kamen

Harland Sanders' dad died when he was five years old.
His family became so poor as a consequence that Harland
Sanders got his first job when he was ten. He was fired.

"It looks like you'll never amount to anything."

— Harland Sander's mother[1]

Harland Sanders, later know as Colonel Sanders, eventually became the founder of the KFC restaurant franchise. There are now over 18,000 KFC restaurants worldwide.[2]

Despite being a hard worker, Colonel Sanders was frequently fired from his jobs: he was fired for insubordination when he was a railway engineer, ended his career as a lawyer in a fistfight with a client, and got canned as an insurance salesman when he refused to turn in his client accounts.

"[Colonel Sanders] ... was temperamentally unsuited to being a paid employee; [Colonel Sanders] had enough chance at being one, enough for two lifetimes, and had failed again and again."

— Josh Ozerky[3]

Colonel Sanders would finally find some business success in a restaurant and gas station in Corbin, Kentucky. But bad luck headed Colonel Sanders way when a new highway was built that bypassed his establishment, drastically reducing the number of customers for his business. He sold his business for very little, leaving Colonel Sanders, at 65 years old, in difficult financial circumstances.

"One has to remember that every failure can be a stepping-stone to something better..."

— Colonel Sanders

How it works for the

Messy Late Bloomer

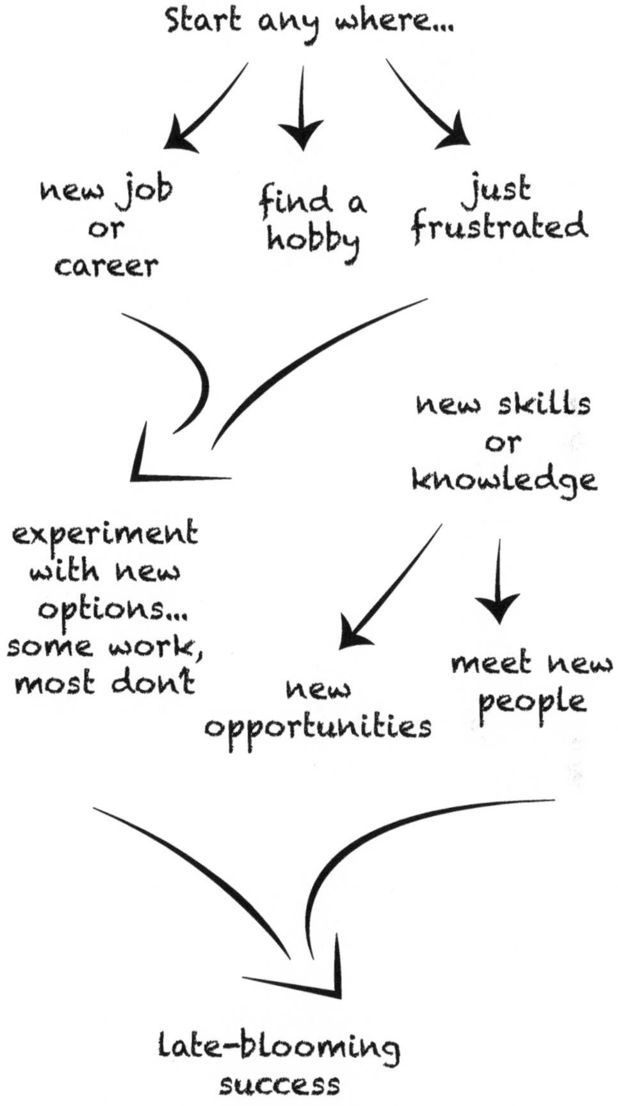

Start any where...

new job
or
career

find a
hobby

just
frustrated

new skills
or
knowledge

experiment
with new
options...
some work,
most don't

new
opportunities

meet new
people

late-blooming
success

Rather than stay home and regret how his business ended, Colonel Sanders decided to focus on selling his popular chicken recipe, that he developed at his former restaurant, through franchise agreements. The Colonel traveled across the United States selling franchises, often sleeping in his car at night to save money. Colonel Sanders became a huge business success.

At 74 years old, Colonel Sanders sold his company for two million dollars. But he continued his role as the ambassador of the KFC restaurants throughout his seventies and eighties. As KFC's spokesman, Colonel Sanders appeared on talk shows, performed in commercials, and gave many presentations. Colonel Sanders throughly enjoyed his later years during which he also spent time raising money for charity and dispensing advice.

Messy Late Bloomers

"You can never learn less: you can only learn more. The reason I know so much is because I have made so many mistakes."

— R. Buckminster Fuller

Colonel Sanders is a classic *Messy Late Bloomer*. Living life provided him with many hard lessons. However, each "failure" provided feedback on how to do things better next time.

For many *Messy Late Bloomers*, it takes decades of real-life education before they have the skills and experience necessary to put together their most valuable work.

Thank goodness Colonel Sanders didn't give up when

he was 65 years old. Think of all the things he would have missed.

Messy Late Bloomers and Business

"We are all faced with a series of great opportunities brilliantly disguised as impossible situations."
—Charles R. Swindoll

Research shows that experiencing a business failure, can actually increase a person's future odds of business success. For example, a study of retail business owners in the State of Texas found that entrepreneurs who had owned a failed retail store, and then started a new business, were more likely to have their new business succeed than entrepreneurs who had never had a business fail.[4] This study is an example of how a "messy" method of progress, including business failures, can be a stepping stone to late-in-life success.

Messy Late Bloomers and the Arts

Particularly shy, with a full beard and small eyes, Paul Cézanne did not look like a genius. Certainly no one who knew Paul Cézanne when he was in his twenties would have predicted that one of his paintings would eventually sell for over two hundred and fifty million dollars.[5] The most ever paid for a painting.

How did Paul Cézanne go from a "failed" painter to a celebrated *Messy Late Bloomer*?

Paul Cézanne started painting almost immediately after he finished his formal schooling. His paintings

The image to the left is a self-portrait completed by Paul Cézanne in 1895, when he was fifty-six years old.

Cézanne is known for being an artistic late bloomer, with all of his best-known works being created later in life.

The Card Players is a series of five paintings completed by Paul Cézanne later in life. One of the paintings in the series was sold for approximately 250 million dollars in 2011.

always looked different compared to other people's paintings. In fact, he had a phase where he painted with the blade of a knife. Paul Cézanne often painted without a specific goal in mind, and kept trying different ways to find the truth in what he saw.

"I could paint for a hundred years, a thousand years, without stopping and I would still feel as though I knew nothing."

— Paul Cézanne

Many of Paul Cézanne's friends did not think much of his career when he was in his forties. Sadly, even his best friend since boyhood, Émile Zola, had lost faith in Paul Cézanne's ability to succeed as a painter.

Émile Zola was an admired author, and he wrote the book, *L'Oeuvre* (*The Work*), about a failed impressionist painter which most people agreed was based on the life of Paul Cézanne. After the publication of the book, Paul Cézanne and Émile Zola stopped speaking, but Paul Cézanne continued to paint.

Paul Cézanne's method of experimenting with different painting techniques, slowly lead him to significantly improve his abilities.

By the time Cézanne was in his fifties, he started to receive public recognition for his work. It was also in the later part of his life that he created his most notable pieces of art.

Messy Late Bloomers and Artistic Research

David Galenson is an economist from the University of

Chicago who has studied artists and their productivity. In particular, he compared the price of various pieces of art with the age of artist when they created the work. Galenson found that there were many artists, such as the sculptor Auguste Rodin and the painter Paul Cézanne, whose most expensive pieces of work were created at older ages.[6]   David Galenson concluded that this was empirical evidence that these artists were getting better at creating art as they got older.

Summary

"Fall seven times, stand up eight."
— Japanese Proverb

The challenge with *Messy Late Bloomers* is that in mid-life they do not seem particularly talented, and that can be terribly discouraging. However, with time, effort and continuous attempts, *Messy Late Bloomers* can create extraordinary success.

Chapter 2
Bad News
Late Bloomers

*"All your problems, discouragements,
and heartaches are, in truth, great
opportunities in disguise."*

— Og Mandino

Madeleine Albright was married for 23 years when her husband asked for a divorce. Her husband had found a younger woman who, he pointed out, was prettier than her.

The divorce took a great toll on Madeleine. But

Madeleine Albright slowly turned this painful experience into motivation to reach higher in her career.

> *"Well into adulthood, I was never*
> *supposed to be what I became."*
> — Madeleine Albright[1]

After her divorce, Madeleine Albright took a job at Georgetown University and put a great deal of energy into helping several politicians with their campaigns. She worked extremely hard.

Madeleine was able to handle her workload because she was no longer married, and did not need to worry about supporting her husband's career. Also, because she was older when the divorce occurred, her children were grown, allowing her to focus more time on her work.

In 1997, Madeleine Albright became the first female Secretary of State for the United States.[2]

> *"When I became Secretary of State,*
> *I realized that ... I would never have*
> *climbed that high had I still been*
> *married."*
> — Madeleine Albright[3]

When Madeleine Albright took a look back on her life in her memoir, she noted the pivotal role her divorce played in her career trajectory. As such, Madeleine is a *Bad News Late Bloomer*, using the pain of her divorce to create late-blooming success.

Bad News Late Bloomers

Harsh life experiences such as a painful divorce, a terrible health diagnosis, or a death in the family are all

How it works for the

Bad News Late Bloomer

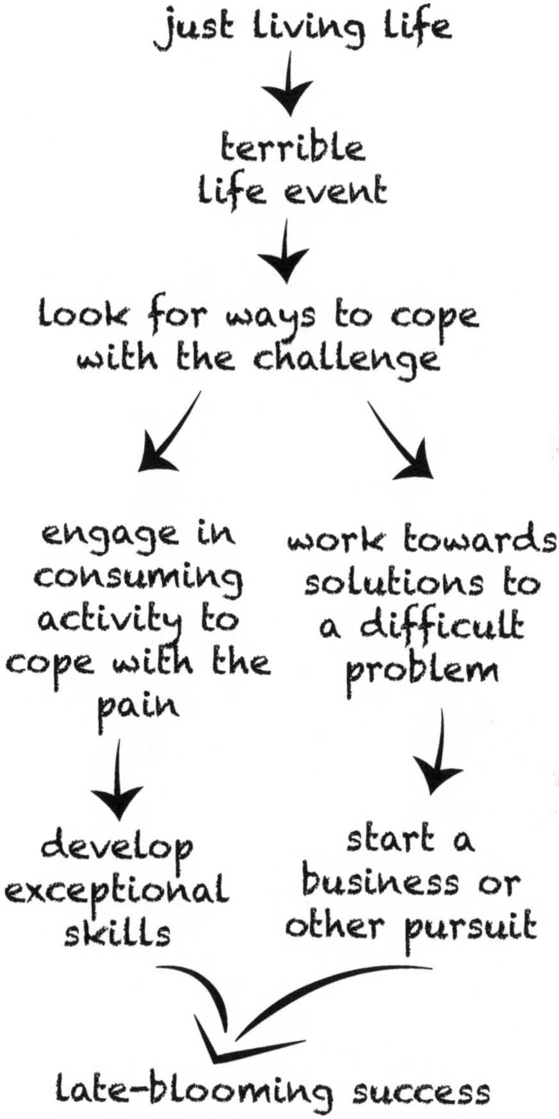

just living life

↓

terrible
life event

↓

look for ways to cope
with the challenge

↙   ↘

engage in   work towards
consuming   solutions to
activity to   a difficult
cope with the   problem
pain

↓   ↓

develop   start a
exceptional   business or
skills   other pursuit

↘↙

late-blooming success

events that can be a catalyst to become a *Bad News Late Bloomer*. Usually, the painful experience creates either one, or both, of the following conditions for the future late bloomer:

1. Motivation to solve a problem; or
2. The need to engage in a consuming activity that helps heal.

We will look at each of these conditions separately.

1. Motivation to Solve a Problem

"A problem is a chance for you to do your best."

— Duke Ellington

Margaret Rudkin's son had asthma. His asthma grew worse if he ate food with artificial preservatives or flavors. Margaret Rudkin started baking wholesome bread that her son could eat comfortably. This was the start of the Pepperidge Farm company.

Pepperidge Farm grew quickly, and by the time Margaret Rudkin was 51 years old the company was producing 50,000 bread loaves each week.[4] Margaret Rudkin later sold Pepperidge Farm to the Campbell Soup Company.

For Margaret Rudkin, the bad news of her son's asthma gave her the motivation to become an extraordinary *Bad News Late Bloomer*.

The desire to solve a problem is an instigating force for many late bloomers, which coupled with hard work, can result in extraordinary success later in life.

2. Engaging in a Consuming Activity

> *"In times of great stress or adversity, it's always best to keep busy, to plow your anger and your energy into something positive."*
>
> — Lee Iacocca

The heartbreak of losing his son and wife caused Fauja Singh to turn to running at 84 years old. He explained in an interview that running was "God's way of distracting me from suffering mentally from the loss..."[5]   Fauja Singh ran his first marathon at age 89, and was the first 100 year old to complete a marathon.[6]

Fauja Singh did not run for fame or to make money. He ran because it helped him cope with the difficult circumstances he was facing. His loss provided him with the need to train for marathons in his 80s, 90s and beyond. However, all of Fauja's running brought him a great deal of fame and the ability to set marathon records — making him an extraordinary late bloomer.

Research Regarding Bad News Late Bloomers

Researchers in the area of human psychology have found that in many cases, people who endure harsh life experiences can create positive change in their lives.

> *"For many persons, the struggle with*

loss and grief can be accompanied by
the experience of positive change, that is,
post-traumatic growth."

— Richard G. Tedeschi
& Lawrence G. Calhoun[7]

When a person experiences a traumatic event, they may implement a positive coping method, or have a change in perspective. The outcome of these positive changes can be transformative. However, these positive experiences do not completely erase the negative impact of the event.

"Both positive experiences and negative
outcomes remain clear in the
experience of people reporting
PTG (post-traumatic growth)."

— Richard G. Tedeschi,
Lawrence G. Calhoun and Arnie Cann[8]

In fact, many late bloomers turn to challenging activities to mitigate how much a loss consumes them. Over time, the proficiency they obtain through this focused activity leads to a level of success they could only dream of at younger ages.

Summary

"If your going through hell,
keep going."

— Winston Churchill

Bad News Late Bloomers are people who face a situation that most people would consider a tragedy. They have a valid reason to pull away from life. But rather than letting negative events permanently shatter their lives, they use the event as a catalyst for undertaking positive endeavors.

Chapter 3
New Stage
Late Bloomers

"You're definitely a different person at different stages in your life."

— Ben Harper

Frank McCourt grew up in a poor Irish slum. He managed to immigrate to New York when he was 19 years old. He became a high school English teacher, and taught in New York for 30 years. However, it was only after Frank McCourt retired from teaching that he completed his finest work, writing the story of his childhood.

Frank McCourt's memoir, titled *Angela's Ashes*, was published when he was 66 years old. The book sold over 10 million copies and has been translated into 25 languages.[1] Frank McCourt also won the Pulitzer Prize for *Angela's Ashes*.

Not one to rest on his laurels, McCourt continued writing, and came out with three more books: *'Tis*, *Teacher Man*, and a children's book *Angela and the Baby Jesus*. Frank McCourt turned his retirement into a time of late-blooming success.

New Stage Late Bloomers

"The undertaking of a new action brings new strength."

— Richard L. Evans

New Stage Late Bloomers look for new challenges as they move to a different stage of life. A new stage can begin at any life transition. There are two stages that are particularly associated with late-blooming success:

1. Unemployment or low employment, and

2. Retirement.

We'll take a quick look at each of these stages and how they can lead to great opportunities.

1. Unemployment or Low Employment

"Change brings opportunity."

— Nido Qubein

There are many people who were fired from their jobs and then moved on to the most notable and successful time of their lives. One example is Michael Bloomberg.

Michael Bloomberg is now a billionaire. But at age 39, he lost his job at Salomon Brothers when it merged

How it works for the

New Stage Late Bloomer

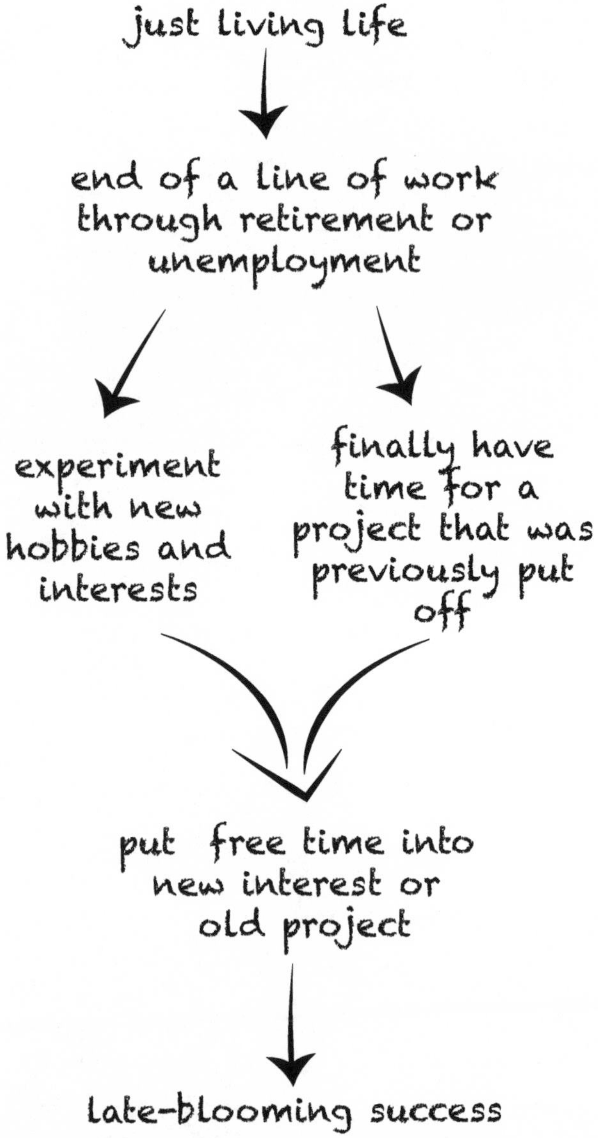

just living life

↓

end of a line of work
through retirement or
unemployment

↓   ↓

experiment
with new
hobbies and
interests

finally have
time for a
project that was
previously put
off

↓

put free time into
new interest or
old project

↓

late-blooming success

with another investment bank.

> *"You can't sit there and worry about everything."*
> — Michael Bloomberg

Bloomberg used his severance package and experience in banking to found a business information company that got its first client when Michael was 40 years old. The business has flourished ever since, bringing Bloomberg a great deal of wealth.

Looking to further contribute to his community, Michael Bloomberg became the Mayor of New York City at 59 years old.

Another person that was spurred on to late-blooming success by a job loss was Raymond Thornton Chandler. Chandler became a mystery writer after losing his job at an oil company when he was forty-four years old.[2] He wrote several successful novels including *The Big Sleep* and *The Long Goodbye*.

2. Retirement

> *"Every new beginning comes from some other beginning's end."*
> — Seneca

Retirement is a particularly interesting time for late bloomers. Retirement can come about in many different ways; it may be forced upon us because of poor health or be actively chosen. While retirement usually gives the gift of time, the gift of financial independence is much more uncertain. Consider the life of Bill Traylor.

Bill Traylor was destitute when he started to create

Peter Roget, above, retired from his career in science at 69 years old. After Roget retired, he put together his most notable and celebrated project the *Roget's Thesaurus*, a book that went on to sell millions of copies.

art. He was 85 years old, no longer able to work, and homeless. Bill Traylor spent his nights sleeping in the back of a funeral home.[3] But his days were spent drawing outside.

Mr. Traylor drew on the back of detergent boxes and on paper bags. Initially, his pictures were very simple. But as he continued to draw, his pictures became more sophisticated. A fellow artist brought him better tools, and soon his art became even more vivid and creative.

Bill Traylor created over a 1,000 works of art.[4] And with all of that creation — skill and mastery was born.

Bill Traylor's artistic accomplishment demonstrates that it is the time available, more than the prospect of financial independence, that makes retirement an important life stage for late bloomers.

> *"Don't simply retire from something;*
> *have something to retire to."*
> — Harry Emerson Fosdick

In retirement, some late bloomers work on a project that they have always wanted to complete, but did not have the time to work on during their working career. Consider the life of Peter Roget.

Sadness and anxiety were deeply interwoven into Peter Roget's life. One way Peter Roget dealt with his feelings was by making lists of words. So when Roget retired from his scientific and medical career when he was 69 years old, he decided that he would turn his word lists into a useful book. After four years of solid work, *Roget's Thesaurus* was published. Peter Roget was 73 years old. *Roget's Thesaurus* has sold over 32 million copies.[5]

Summary

"What I love best in life is new starts."
— Karl Lagerfeld

New stages in life can lead to late-blooming success. In particular, retirement or a period of unemployment can be a great opportunity. However, it is not necessary that a new stage be perfectly arranged with deep financial means and good health. Rather, it is simply the fact that there is time to dedicate to a new form of work that is essential to becoming a late bloomer. *New Stage Late Bloomers* put their energies into making the next step of their lives meaningful.

Section Two

• • •

The Advantages of Aging

Chapter 4
The Experience
Advantage

hard
knocks

*"The only source of knowledge is
experience."*

— Albert Einstein

Laura Ingalls learned needed to start working early in life
to help her family. She became a teacher at 15 years
old. After she married Almanzo Wilder (becoming Laura
Ingalls Wilder), she dedicated her life to the hard work of
being a farmer's wife.

Her early married life was fraught with many
difficulties. She was heart broken by the loss of her
newborn son.[1] Her husband Almazo became seriously
ill, and even after recovering, always walked with a cane

after his illness. Moreover, a terrible multi-year drought left Laura and her husband deep in debt because they could not produce any wheat crops.[2]

Laura and her husband moved several times after this challenging period. When they settled down again, it was in Missouri on Rocky Ridge Farm. They had learned from their experience of a long-term drought and became diversified farmers.

Laura started writing part-time for the *Missouri Ruralist* to supplement her income. Her interest in writing deepened over time. In particular, she began working on her memoirs in her sixties.

Wilder's memoir was repeated rejected by publishers. But Wilder solicited feedback as to why publishers didn't like her work. In response to publisher's suggestions, she repackaged her memoirs as work of fiction written for children. She changed some of the book's characters and left out some of the hardships she and her family faced.

This new version of her book was published under the title, *Little House in The Big Woods*, when Wilder was 65 years old. She went on to write seven more books in the series, and won five Newberry Honors for exceptional Children's literature.[3] The books were also made into the popular TV series *Little House on the Prairie* starring Melissa Gilbert and Michael Landon.

Wilder used her many diverse life experiences to later create her own late-blooming success as a writer.

Experience Advantage

There are several different ways that late bloomers, like Laura Ingalls Wilder, may leverage their life experiences to become a late bloomer including:

1. Using experience as a building block to a new career;

2. Using experience to improve a skill set.

Let's look at each of these situations in turn.

1. Experience as a Building Block to a New Career

"A mind that is stretched by a new experience can never go back to its old dimensions."

— Oliver Wendell Holmes

Life experience can often be a source of inspiration for a second career as an artist or writer. For example, it was the extensive pioneer and farming experiences that Wilder lived through that gave her the content for her successful series of children's books.

But, Laura Ingalls Wilder is not alone. In fact, many late bloomers integrated their life experiences into a new career as an artist. Perhaps this is part of the reason there are so many late blooming artists (check out the late-blooming lists from pages 119 to 127).

However, life experience is an advantage in many different careers. Consider how Wally Blume translated his experience in the food industry into a career as an ice cream entrepreneur.

Wally Blume worked in the dairy industry for decades. He had experience working at a supermarket, doing sales and marketing for a dairy, and as a salesman for an ice cream company.[4]

In his late fifties, Wally and a partner had a terrific idea for an ice cream flavor called Moose Tracks — which included vanilla ice cream, fudge and peanut butter cups. He pursued the business opportunity because his extensive experience gave him the confidence in the concept:

> *"I had been in the business for 30 years*
> *and had a pretty good feel for what*
> *worked and what didn't work."*

— Wally Blume[5]

Wally Blume's company, Delani Flavors, became very successful, doing millions of dollar in sales each year.[6]

2. Experience Improves a Skill Set

> *"You don't learn to walk by following*
> *rules. You learn by doing,*
> *and by falling over."*

— Richard Branson

Japanese artist Katsushika Hokusai was born into poverty in Japan. He initially worked polishing mirrors, and as an engraver for a bookshop.[7] Hokusai eventually got an artistic mentor and began his professional drawing career.

Soon Hokusai's curiosity in diverse drawing styles drew him off of his professional track. In fact, he needed to complement his career by selling things such as peppers and calenders. However, he continued to draw every day and his skills became more exceptional as the years passed.

Hokusai himself observed:

> *"I drew some pictures I thought fairly*
> *good when I was fifty, but really nothing*
> *I did before the age of seventy was of*

Katsushika Hokusai drew this self-portrait of himself when he was 78 years old.

Hokusai was known for completing many of his most famous works later in life.

He was an enthusiastic life-long student of his craft.

Katsushika Hokusai made many of his best drawings later in life including his famous series *Thirty-six Views of Mount Fiji*. The image above, is part of that series. The picture is of Mount Fuji as it reflects in Lake Kawaguchi.

*any value at all. At seventy-three I have
at last caught every aspect of nature
— birds, fish, animals, insects, trees,
grassess, all. When I am eighty I shall
have developed still further…"*

—Katsushika Hokusai[8]

Hokusai's worked with a great deal of dedication to improve his skills over the span of decades. In fact, he created more than 30,000 paintings and drawings over his lifetime.

So, it comes as no surprise that Hokusai is considered to have done his best work later in life including his world-famous drawings *Thirty-six Views of Mount Fuji.*[9] This series of drawings capture Japan's most significant and sacred mountain. Hokusai didn't even begin working on this set of drawings until he was in his sixties.

As Hokusai's life shows, getting older provides the opportunity to continually refine and improve a late bloomer's skills. A person's best work does not necessarily happen in their twenties, but often only after decades of hard work and experience.

Summary

*"Nothing is a waste of time if you use the
experience wisely."*

— Auguste Rodin

Late bloomers often see aging as an advantage because of the increase in the range and depth of their experiences. These extensive life experiences can help build a bridge to late-blooming success through improvement in a late bloomer's skills, or by providing a source of inspiration, and a reservoir of knowledge, to engage in a new field of work.

Chapter 5
The Perspective
Advantage

"Life gets more interesting as it goes on. It becomes fuller because there is perspective there."

— Ann Dowd

R. Buckminster "Bucky" Fuller had some difficult years early on. He was expelled from college twice. And in his thirties, he became deeply depressed when his daughter died, and his troubles were further compounded by great financial difficulties. Fuller didn't even know if he wanted to go on.

But a change in perspective — changed his life.

Fuller decided to dedicate his life to the service of others and "discover what the little, penniless, unknown individual might be able to do effectively on behalf of all humanity."[1]

> *"I'm not a genius. I'm just a tremendous*
> *bundle of experience."*
> — R. Buckminster Fuller

Fuller went on to write over 30 books, have 25 United States patents and be awarded a multitude of honorary doctoral degrees.[2]   Clearly, making life a learning experiment filled with purpose was a beneficial change in perspective for this late bloomer.

The Perspective Advantage

So how is it that improved perspective through increased age can help late bloomers succeed?   Well, there are several ways.

1. Perspective helps a person focus on what is really important; and

2. Perspective helps improve the quality of a person's work.

Let's look at each of these topics individually.

1. Perspective and Focusing on What is Important

> *"At the center of your being you have the*
> *answer; you know who you are and you*
> *know what you want."*
> — Lao Tzu

John Mahony became an internationally known actor when he landed the role as Martin Krane in the hit TV show *Fraser* at 53 years old.[3] What many people don't know is that before Mahony became an actor, he was actually the editor of a medical journal. But Mahony had doubts about his editing job, he began to wonder:

> *"Is this going to be it for me, am I going to be spending the rest of my life writing about cataracts and hemorrhoids?"*

> — John Mahony[4]

John Mahony knew he was unhappy and needed to make a change. He asked himself the "big" questions, which got him to take action towards his dreams. In Mahony's case, changing his career from medical editor to actor.

As people age, they often become more thoughtful about whether they feel fulfilled. This tendency toward self-reflection as people get older, can improve a person's self-knowledge and ability to make quality choices.

Moreover, just by living life, people learn to better understand what makes them happy, or miserable. Combining this information, with the greater perspective developed with age, helps expand a person's perspective on the purpose of their lives.

This improved perspective can lead to making better decisions on what career or project to spend time on.

2. Perspective and quality of work

> *"I have been to Hell and back and let me tell you it was wonderful. "*

> — Louise Bourgeois

Louise Bourgeois was a sculptor most of her life. Her difficult childhood led her to explore many different themes regarding domesticity, family and feminism in her work. She did this through the development of several series of sculptures.

Interestingly, Bourgeios brought an increasing amount of richness and perspective to her sculptures over time.

> *"One must accept the fact that others*
> *don't see what you do."*
>
> — Louise Bourgeois

In fact, Bourgeois created her most famous series of sculptures in her eighties. It included a giant spider sculpture titled Maman (which was over 9 meters high), which was meant to honor here mother.[5]

Like Louis Bourgeois, time and perspective can be powerful tools for many late bloomers. As a person ages, they are able to process their unique experiences against the backdrop of the knowledge they have accumulated about life.

For some individuals, this process of cultivating perspective can take a long time. For example, Harry Bernstein who wrote his best-selling memoir the *Invisible Wall* in his 90s noted in an interview:

> *"If I had not lived until I was 90, I would*
> *not have been able to write this book… It*
> *just could not have been done even when*
> *I was 10 years younger. I wasn't ready."*
>
> — Harry Bernstien[6]

It was the self-knowledge and perspective that Harry Bernstein achieved at 90 years old that made his book possible.

Summary

"If you change the way you look at things, the things you look at change."
— Wayne Dyer

As we get older, our perspective about our lives, skills and goals expands. This improved perspective can help us make better choices and create more compelling work — which helps create late-blooming success.

Chapter 6
The Mindful
Advantage

"Life gives you plenty of time to do whatever you want to do if you stay in the present moment."

— Deepak Chopra

Nelson Mandela became the President of the Republic of South Africa when he was 75 years old. Mandela used his extraordinary political and relationship skills to negotiate an end to apartheid and create many initiatives to heal a nation that had been segregated for decades.

Mandela displayed such extraordinary skills in bringing about change he won a Nobel Peace prize and become internationally acclaimed.

Wisdom

"A good head and a good heart are always a formidable combination."

— Nelson Mandela

Prior to becoming President, Nelson Mandela was a political prisoner for 27 years. He endured deep unfairness and difficult living conditions. But when Mandela became President of South Africa, he chose not to seek revenge for his imprisonment, and rather dedicated his energies to healing the racial divides in his country. Nelson Mandela had achieved a deep state of wisdom about what would help his nation.

But what is wisdom? Wisdom can be thought of a method of thinking which gives a person a better appreciation as to how life works. It can include many factors such as:

- an ability to see other people's point of view;

- an ability to predict and manage social situations; and

- an ability to apply extensive life experience to better understand different contexts.[1]

But there is more to wisdom then these factors. *Psychology Today* provides a thoughtful definition of wisdom that many people would agree with:

"[wisdom] involves an integration of knowledge, experience, and deep understanding that incorporates

tolerance for the uncertainties of life as well as its ups and downs. There's an awareness of how things play out over time, and it confers a sense of balance."

— *Psychology Today*[2]

The sophisticated reasoning that accompanies wisdom take time to develop. This is why older people are more likely to be considered wise. However, aging is not a guarantee of increased wisdom. As noted psychologist Erik Erikson noted:

"Lots of old people don't get wise, but you don't get wise unless you age."

— Erik Erikson

With increasing age, many people become wiser because they integrate their life experiences into their decision making processes.

People who become wiser with age, often become more successful as they are better at predicting the outcomes of a range of business, cultural and social situations; and can adjust their actions accordingly.

Less Negative Emotional Reactivity

"Mature workers are less impulsive, less reactive, more creative and more centered."

— Deepak Chopra

Another reason why aging can be an advantage to creating success is that older people are often calmer in the face of negative circumstances.

For example, in a study conducted by Professor Susan Charles from the University of California found that when faced with a negative social situation, older adults become less angry and upset about the situation than younger people.[3] In particular, Charles and her team conducted an interesting experiment where they had people listen to tapes of other people who seemed to be making unfavorable remarks about them, and then the subjects would talk about how they felt. Older people were consistently less upset then younger people about the negative comments.[4]

This observation, that older people tend to react less strongly than younger people to negative situations, has be observed across numerous other studies as well.[5] Although, there is not a consensus as to why this trend is observed. Some researchers feel that the older brain simply reacts less to certain negative situations, while other researchers think that there are specific coping strategies used by older people to feel less intense negative emotions.[6]

No matter the why, the ability of older people to manage (or feel less) negative emotions is a great advantage for late bloomers. Any attempt to achieve a desired goal is filled with many obstacles and difficult situations. If the late bloomer can maintain a better perspective on a difficult situation, they are more likely to achieve a satisfactory resolution to the situation.

Summary

*"The capacity to ride out emotional
storms more flexibly and resiliently is*

one of the great fruits of aging."

— Gene D. Cohen

Age can be a terrific advantage to achieving late-blooming success because with age often comes wisdom. Also, as people get older, they become more capable of staying calm during negative situations, which can be a great advantage for a late bloomer.

Section Three

...

Common Components of Late-Blooming Success

Chapter 7
Internal Motivation

*"Motivation is the power
that creates action."*

— Tamara Lowe

Divorced and broke, Louise Nevelson's life looked bleak to outsiders when she was in her thirties. But Louise Nevelson was doing the one thing she really wanted to do — creating art.

*"... even if I didn't sell my work, I still
felt like a winner."*

— Louise Nevelson

Louise Nevelson would not have become a late bloomer without her internal motivation to sustain her. In fact, Louise Nevelson only discovered her preferred artistic medium of sculpture in her thirties, and spent years barely scraping by financially as she focused on building her sculptures.

When Louise Nevelson was in her forties, her work slowly gained recognition, with showings in galleries. Although, she still struggled financially.

In her fifties, Louise Nevelson seemed to have turned a corner towards a sustainable art career. However, in her early sixties a bad deal with a gallery and an extravagant exhibition that resulted in nonexistent sales, forced Nevelson to sell her home and put her into a financial meltdown. Most of her colleagues thought that her "moment" had passed.[1]

> *"I wanted this [art], and I felt rich*
> *enough to pay the price."*
> — Louise Nevelson

But not motivated by money, but rather her internal desire to create art, Louise Nevelson continued to work. Much of her new art sold and she managed to buy back her home. By the time Louise reached her seventies, her career was in full bloom with awards, exhibitions and sales in plentiful supply. Moreover, Louise Nevelson started working on commissioned outdoor monuments in her early seventies, during which she successfully switched the medium that she used to build her sculptures.

Louise Nevelson worked up until her death at eighty-eight years of age. She is remembered as one of America's best sculptors because of the work she did later in life.

Internal Motivation

"Each day becomes more meaningful,
and your life is enhanced when your
actions are guided by what
inspires you."
— Bernie Siegel

When a person is internally motivated they can enjoy the process of working, even if external rewards are not readily available. For example, a person can enjoy completing a painting on a canvas, even when no one buys the painting.

But if someone paints only to make money, then when their paintings do not sell, they are more likely to throw in the towel. Because it can take a long time for late bloomers to become recognized for their work, it is critical that they find their work personally rewarding.

No one becomes a late bloomer doing something they hate.

External Motivation

"Just when I think I have learned the
way to live, life changes."
— Hugh Prather

Wanting external rewards such as enough income to buy a home is normal. Late bloomers are not immune to these motivating factors. They are simply internally motivated as well. The balance between internal and external motivation is unique to each late bloomer.

To make an interesting comparison to Louise Nevelson's powerful internal motivation, let us take a

Auguste Rodin (1840 – 1917) is one of the world's most famous sculptors. The first twenty years of his career were spent working as a craftsman for other sculptors.

The Thinker (1879–1889) seen here to the left is one of Rodin's most famous sculptures. It is recognized worldwide.

look at the life of another sculptor, Auguste Rodin.

Rodin was highly motivated to become an artist and a sculptor. However, he also wanted to make a decent living from the beginning of his career. So, Auguste Rodin spent the first 20 years of his career working as a craftsman for other sculptors; this meant he spent most of his time creating sculptures that someone else designed and signing their name to the piece.

Rodin would later become one of the most famous sculptors of all time because once he managed to achieve some of his external financial goals, he spent the majority of his time and energy creating his own sculptures.

Some of Auguste Rodin's most famous sculptures include *Monument to Balzac*, *The Burghers of Calais*, and *The Thinker*.

Motivation to Work or Retire

One place where internal and external motivators can lead a potential late bloomer off track is when the decision to retire from a specific career is thought of as a decision to completely stop working.

> *"You can retire from a job, but don't ever retire from making extremely meaningful contributions in life."*
> — Stephen Covey

Wanting to quit a job, or retire from a career, is often not synonymous with not wanting to work. In fact, research has demonstrated that even within a particular job, motivation levels will vary by the specific task.[2] For example, while a person may not be motivated to attend meetings, they may be motivated to write blog posts. Therefore, it is valuable to recognize that a desire to retire from a specific career, does not automatically imply a lack of motivation to work.

Many late bloomers retire from a specific career and continue to work on projects they enjoy and find internally motivating. Perhaps, this is why there are so many *New Stage Late Bloomers* (Chapter 3) who find their most meaningful success in retirement.

Summary

"Success is almost totally dependent upon drive and persistence. The extra energy required to make another effort or try another approach is the secret of winning."
— Denis Waitley

Late bloomers usually need to be internally motivated, so that they continue to enjoy working even when they don't receive external rewards. However, late bloomers can still have a plethora of external motivators such as money or recognition.

Moreover, many late bloomers who are no longer motivated by their career, still have their own internal motivation to complete meaningful projects.

Chapter 8
Master a Skill

"Success is a by-product of excellence."

— Deepak Chopra

Harry Bernstein was devastated when his wife died. To help him cope, the 93 year old wrote *The Invisible Wall*, which is a memoir about his childhood. The book became a huge success. It was published when Mr. Bernstein was 96 years old. When you read the book, you can tell that Harry Bernstein is a skilled writer.

Mastering a skill is a crucial part of becoming a late bloomer. In Mr. Bernstein's case, his writing skills did not just appear at age 93. Harry Bernstein had practiced writing in different ways during his life including writing freelance articles and working as an editor for a construction magazine.

Like many late bloomers, Harry Bernstein slowly mastered his craft, so that at age 93, he was able to create his best work.

> *"My 90s were the most productive*
> *years of my life."*
> — Harry Bernstein

However, Harry Bernstein's long-term mastery of a skill is only one method to late blooming success. Another strategy is to apply skills that you have gathered over time, none of which are at the level of mastery, in a unique way (for more about this see Chapter 6: Unique Skill Set).

Learning New Skills

> *"Everyone has a chance to learn,*
> *improve, and build up their skills."*
> — Tom Peters

Adults can learn and master new skills. But the news actually gets better, older adults can actually grow their brains.

Researchers from two leading German universities taught a group of older adults how to juggle over a three-month period. The researchers also had a control group that did not learn how to juggle. The researchers did a MRI scan of the study participants' brains before and after they learned to juggle. The study found that there was an increase in the gray matter in the brains of those people who learned how to juggle, but not for the people in the control group.[1] This means the adult participants' brains had literally grown to learn the new skill.

Don't believe the conventional wisdom that learning

can not happen when you are older — it is not true, and there is the science to prove it.

Making Learning Skills Easier

"... there is all kinds of proof that exercise, both physical and mental, increases brain activity."

— Nolan Bushnell

There are several ways that potential late bloomers can make it easier for themselves to learn and master the skills they need to succeed. In fact, studies into adult learning indicates there are several strategies that can be highly beneficial including:

1. Participating in cardiovascular exercise;

2. Engaging in cognitively challenging activities; and,

3. Practicing the skill you want to develop.

Let us take a more detailed look at each of these three strategies.

1. Cardiovascular Exercise

If you want to make learning a new skill easier, consider going to the gym. Research has found that aerobic exercise — the kind of exercise that gets your heart pumping — can literally increase the size of a person's brain[2] — making learning easier and your memory sharper.

In one study, researchers recruited 120 older adults and divided them into two groups. One group was assigned a stretching class, while the other group did an aerobic exercise class that would get their heart pumping. MRI imaging showed that the aerobic exercise participants increased the size of their hippocampus (the part of the brain that processes information).[3] However, the stretching group did not see any growth in their brains.

So if you think you can't be a late bloomer because you don't feel sharp, try going to the gym. Another benefit of aerobic exercise is that it will improve your general endurance, so that you can keep up with your desire to learn, and your need to practice.

2. Cognitively Challenging Activities

"Our brains renew themselves throughout life to an extent previously thought not possible."

— Michael Gazzaniga

The kind of activities you engage in, can affect your ability to stay sharp and learn new skills.

There are many different kinds of "brain" enhancing activities that can help you cultivate your ability to learn. For example, a study published in the *New England Journal of Medicine* identified doing crosswords frequently and reading regularly help maintain mental sharpness.[4]

Interestingly, researchers have found that playing certain video games may also help late bloomers stay sharp. In fact, professors at North Carolina State University had one group of adults play a virtual-online game called *World of Warcraft* for two weeks;

and they had a second group of adults who did not play the computer game. Participants who played *World of Warcraft* showed a significant improvement on several mental tests compared to the non-playing group.[5]

Late bloomers who are looking to make learning a skill easier should seriously consider engaging in challenging leisure activities to help keep their mind fresh and ready learn new skills

3. Practice, Practice and More Practice

*"It's never crowded along
the extra mile."*

— Wayne Dyer

Practice is the best way to improve a specific skill. Consider the story of Diana Nyad. At age 29, Diana Nyad attempted to swim from Cuba to Florida without using a shark cage. She failed.[6] And shortly after that, Diana retired from competitive swimming. But at age 60, Diana Nyad decided to try again for her dream goal — being the first person to swim from Cuba to Florida without using a shark cage.

Four years after setting her inspirational goal, Diana swam from Florida to Cuba without a shark cage at age 64.[7] Her journey was filled with extensive training. In particular, she built up her swimming endurance gradually with longer and longer swims.

What would have happened if Diana Nyad simply tried to swim from Cuba to Florida without practicing her swimming? She would have failed, of course. Or what if Diana Nyad practiced her swimming, but only for a few days before her undertaking? This wouldn't have worked either.

Diana Nyad was able to complete her historic swim because of the time and effort she dedicated to practicing swimming, as well as being willing to make multiple attempts to swim from Cuba to Florida.

The beauty of this real life example is that it shows how practice can develop extraordinary physical abilities in older age — a level of physical endurance that we might not even have had when we were younger.

Not All Practice is the Same

"It is clear that the vast majority of active individuals spend very little if any time on deliberate practice."

— K. Anders Ericsson and Neil Charness[8]

When a person wants to be a late bloomer, they need to deliberately practice the skill they want to excel at, just like Diana Nyad. Most adults do not put the effort into deliberate practice. If you want to become a late bloomer, deliberate practice is a tool you can use to stand out from the crowd.

Effective deliberate practice needs to be two things:

1. Challenging practice where the person is working to improve; and,

2. Sustained over a long period of time.[9]

Another way of further appreciating the role that practice has on a person's level of ability, is to look at what happens when a person of high ability stops practicing — their skill level tends to decline. For example, researcher Ralf T. Kampe found that the best way to predict how well accomplished pianists play in older age is to know how much they practice. The less they practiced, the worse they got over time.[10]

> *"The path to mastery — becoming ever
> better at something you care about — is
> not lined with daises and spanned by a
> rainbow. If it were more of us would take
> the trip. Mastery hurts."*
>
> — David Pink[11]

Late bloomers do the practice that being extraordinary requires.

What About Talent?

It is common for a person to not bother practicing a skill because they don't believe they have talent. However, research suggests that a lot of what we used to consider inborn talent is rather the outcome of ongoing deliberate practice.[12]

> *"Talent is not a thing; it's a process."*
>
> — David Shenk[13]

In fact, Dr. K. Andes Ericsson, a professor at Florida State University, discovered that much of a person's talent could be predicted by the amount of time the person dedicated to deliberate practice.[14]

Belief and Improvement

> *"... the view you adopt for yourself
> profoundly affects the way you
> lead your life."*
>
> — Carol S. Dweck[15]

An important part of becoming a late bloomer is viewing abilities or skills as something that can be developed over time. In fact, researcher Dr. Carol Dweck, a professor at Stanford University, found that people who believe that ability is developed by practice and effort, tend to be much more successful than those who think that talent is innate.[16] This is because when encountering a serious challenge, people who believe their ability is developed by practice often work harder to develop the skills necessary to master the difficult circumstances, while people who think talent is innate often just give up. Since life is full of challenges, thinking of skills as something that can be improved and developed over time becomes highly beneficial in the long run.

Summary

"Hope begins in the dark, the stubborn hope that if you just show up and try to do the right thing, the dawn will come. You wait and watch and work: you don't give up."

—Anne Lamott

Mastering a skill is one way to become a late bloomer. It takes a great deal of time, energy and practice to master a skill. However, you can help yourself learn by exercising, engaging in challenging cognitive activities, and practicing the skill you want to improve.

Chapter 9
Unique Skill Set

"My combined mediocre skills are worth far more than the sum of the parts. If you think extraordinary talent and a magical pursuit of excellence are necessary for success, I say that's just one approach, and probably the hardest. When it comes to skills, quantity often beats quality."

— Scott Adams[1]

Julia Child really hit her stride in her fifties when she began hosting a cooking show. Sharing her sense of humor, cooking skills, and impressive presentation skills with the public is what made her an extraordinary late bloomer.

Julia Child took a long time to discover and cultivate her perfect skill set. Her journey began when she was looking for something to occupy her time in France while her husband was working. First, Julia took a course in making hats, but the work did not inspire her.[2] Next, Julia Child enrolled in the Le Cordon Blue, a prestigious French cooking school; at 38 years old, she had finally found part of her calling.

Ms. Child's expanding knowledge and passion for French cooking lead to a joint cookbook project with two other ladies, which eventually became the classic best-selling book, *Mastering the Art of French Cooking*. The book was published when Julie Child was 49 years old. After the book came out, Julia started teaching cooking on television.

Julia Child certainly was not the best chef out there. But her ability to combine her skills effectively made her a successful late bloomer.

Put It Together

Like Julia Child, many late bloomers are not complete masters at one skill. Rather they inspire respect and appreciation by the way they combine their skills to create something meaningful.

"... I'm sort of a generalist."
— Julia Child

It can take time for a late bloomer to figure out what combination of skills they have that would create an interesting product or experience for others. Age and experience often work in a late bloomer's favor as most people develop many different skills over time.

Usually discovering a unique skill set isn't something that happens quickly or easily. Finding a meaningful combination of skills takes work. Below are four strategies that late bloomers use to find their unique skill set:

1. Focus on solving a problem;

2. Brainstorm new skill combinations;

3. Consider your personal style; and

4. Learn a new skill, to add to your skill set.

Let's look at each strategy in a bit more detail.

1. Focus on Solving a Problem

A unique skill set will often come together if you are trying to solve a complicated problem. Consider Momofuke Ando who helped solve Japan's food shortage after World War II by inventing "instant noodles."

Momofuke Ando had some sharp ups and downs. He went to jail for two years for not paying taxes; and he went bankrupt because of his directorship on the board of a credit union.[3] But he applied his creativity, culinary skills, and his messily-learned business skills to invent and sell "instant noodles" at age 48 and "cup of noodles" at age 61.[4]

Momofuke Ando became a billionaire — and more importantly — provided affordable food to millions of people.

2. Brainstorm New Skill Combinations

*"The way to get good ideas is to get lots
of ideas and throw the bad ones away."*

— Linus Pauling

It may be helpful to brainstorm new ways you can combine your current skills. Record all of your ideas without judgment, and then once you are out of new ideas go back and take a look to see if any of the combinations that you thought up are worth trying.

A more paced version of brainstorming is advocated by creativity expert Julia Cameron. She recommends people write "morning pages" every day to stimulate creative ideas in any area of life.[5] Writing or journaling a bit everyday can slowly stirs up ideas, and be a meaningful way to start exploring new combinations of skills.

3. Consider Your Personal Style

*"Always be yourself, express yourself,
have faith in yourself, do not go out and
look for a successful personality and
duplicate it."*

— Bruce Lee

Infusing your personality into something is an act of creativity, and valuable way to broaden your own unique skill set. Clara Peller is a good example.

Clara Peller became an actress in her eighties.[6] She was signed by an agency because of her feisty and forthright manner.[7] Her personality made her delivery of lines, when acting, creative. She was best known for her role in a Wendy's restaurant commercial, her now famous line was "Where's the beef?"

Consider how you can integrate your personality into an area of expertise to enhance your skill set.

4. Learn a New Skill

> *"I am always ready to learn although I*
> *do not always like being taught."*
> — Winston Churchill

It may be the case that after trying several different methods to determine your unique skill set, you still may come up empty. If this is the case, it may be time to learn another skill that you can throw into the mix.

Remember Julia Child? She needed to learn how to cook to become a late bloomer. Then when she combined her cooking skills, with her sense of humor, and relaxed presentation skills, she became an exceptional late bloomer.

Summary

> *"Always remember that you are*
> *absolutely unique. Just like*
> *everyone else."*
> — Margaret Mead

Many people become late bloomers by putting together a unique skill set. Therefore, aspiring late bloomers may want to consider what unique skill set they have to offer. This task can require a great deal of work, time, and creativity. But the results are usually more than worth the effort.

Chapter 10
Key Relationships

"... no one — not rock stars, not professional athletes, not software billionaires, and not even geniuses — ever makes it alone."

— Malcolm Gladwell[1]

Maya Angelou had a childhood filled with poverty, abuse, and dislocation. Her long journey from this painful beginning to a career as an award-winning author, poet and teacher is chronicled in her famous autobiographies including *I Know Why the Caged Bird Sings*, *Gather Together in My Name*, and *The Heart of a Woman*.

One of the most salient themes in Maya Angelou's life was how she managed to build friendships which lead to many new opportunities. Of course, Maya Angelou rose to these opportunities with the skills, hard work and heart that was necessary for her exemplary success; whether it was coordinating a fundraising event for Martin Luther King, or writing an exceptional autobiography.

> *"I have a feeling that I make a very good friend, and I'm a good mother, and a good sister, and a good citizen. I am involved in life itself — all of it."*
> — Maya Angelou

Even well after her success made her a household name, Maya's strong friendships were a central part of her life and career, and she strove to give opportunities to others.

Fellowship and support

> *"The concept of reaching out to others for support isn't about changing who you are. It's about enlisting the help and advice of others to help you become who you can be."*
> — Keith Ferrazzi

Finding people who have similar work interests or goals can be very beneficial for late bloomers. These friends and mentors can provide the support and guidance late bloomers need to move their work forward.

For example, well before she wrote her autobiography, Maya Angelou joined the *Harlem Writers Guild* on the recommendation of her friend James Baldwin, a successful novelist. By attending the Guild, she received feedback on her writing and cultivated her impressive literary skills.

Fellowship can also lead to opportunities. Maya Angelou shared her life story with Jules and Judy Feiffer, the hosts of a dinner party she attended. Judy Feiffer then shared Maya Angelou's story with Robert Loomis from Random House, eventually resulting in Maya Angelou's first published autobiography.[2]

Finding important, or "lucky" opportunities through friends is actually quite common. In fact, British researcher Dr. Richard Wiseman found that lucky people tend to have a "network of luck," or in other words, they know many people who can help them find a chance opportunity.[3]

> *"Sometimes, idealistic people are put off the whole business of networking as something tainted by flattery and the pursuit of selfish advantage. But virtue in obscurity is rewarded only in Heaven. To succeed in this world you have to be known to people."*
>
> — Sonia Sotomayor

Building up friendships and meeting new people is an important part of creating late-blooming success because it is often through these relationships that important chance opportunities arise.

Fellowship and Working Longer

Architect Frank Lloyd Wright began designing the Museum of Modern Art in New York City when he was 76 years old; he worked on the project until his death at 92 years old.[4] It was likely the most creative and acclaimed building of his entire career.

> *"The longer I live,*
> *the more beautiful life becomes."*
> — Frank Lloyd Wright

Architects, like Frank Lloyd Wright, are a group of professionals where late-blooming success is common. There are several possible reasons for this:

- First, the process of designing and constructing buildings is complicated and therefore it takes a long time for people to master all the skills needed to design a truly great building.

- Second, architects usually work with large teams of people. Therefore, the primary architect can lean on many people to complete various aspects of the work. The fellowship involved in the work allows the architect to focus on their strengths.

Film directors, like architects, often find themselves in a similar late-blooming situation for the same two reasons that architects do — the complicated nature of their work, and the fact they work in teams. A great example is Manoel de Oliveira.

Manoel de Oliveira was a Portuguese filmmaker. He made short films and documentaries for decades with limited success. So, he needed to spend much of his life working at his family's business.

Manoel de Oliveira's first "widely successful" movie, *Past and Present*, was produced when he was 63 years old.[5] He increased the number and frequency of the films he made after this — winning awards and recognition worldwide. And Manoel de Oliveira continued to work very hard into old age. In fact, the majority of his movies were made after he was 70 years old.[6]

Manoel was still making movies when he was over a hundred years old. When he was 106 (the year he died) he was thought to be the oldest working man ever.[7]

Fellowship for a Cause

*"As you grow older, you will discover
that you have two hands, one for helping
yourself, the other for helping others."*
— Audrey Hepburn

Cultivating relationships with people in your community to support a worthwhile cause can often be the start of a late-blooming journey.

Consider the life of Marjorie Stoneman Douglas who became an environmental crusader at 79 years old.[8] Her ability to connect with people though her speeches and conversations helped conserve the Florida Everglades and limit development on this environmentally sensitive area.

Marjorie's early life was full of challenges. She married Kenneth Douglas, who turned out to be a con man. In fact, her husband tried to scam her father out of money. This resulted in their divorce. Marjorie Stoneman Douglas also had three nervous breakdowns — the last one after the death of her father.[9]

However, Douglas recovered and wrote many stories and several books. One of the books, *River of Grass*, was about the Florida Everglades. This book would eventually pave the way for her environmental activism. But it was her skill convincing people to protect the natural environment and join her organization *Friends of the Everglades* that made her an extraordinary late bloomer.

Marjorie Stoneman Douglas was awarded the Presidential Medal of Freedom for her work. She continued her environmental activism until she died at 108 years old.[10]

Summary

"Success comes when people act together; failure tends to happen alone."

— Deepak Chopra

A successful late bloomer usually has help along the way. Building relationships with people who have similar interests can be the very thing a late bloomer needs to achieve their goals.

Chapter II
Getting & Using
Feedback

"We all need people who will give us feedback. That's how we improve."

— Bill Gates

Cora Tsouflidou was burnt-out in her late thirties. She was a single mom who had three children and worked punishing hours managing a Greek restaurant. Her body gave out and her mind demanded rest. She describes her situation in her book *Breakfast with Cora*:

> *"It took a long time for me to heal.*
> *Sometimes, I would spend the whole day*

*asleep on the sofa. Then, peacefully, I
decided to stop trying to figure out what
was happening to me; I let go and finally
found the strength to concentrate on
what would really make me happy."*

— Cora Tsouflidou[1]

What Cora Tsouflidou did was inspired and practical. First, she took the exhaustion she felt, and learned to focus on doing what made her happy to recover. She started to write, and doodle drawings. Then, she came up with an idea for a place to eat with a sun as part of the logo. That was the beginning of Cora's — a breakfast and lunch restaurant that now has 130 locations.[2]

Feedback

*"Feedback is the breakfast of
champions."*

— Ken Blanchard

Feedback is the information that tells you how you're are doing. When feedback is positive, it is easy to appreciate. Unfortunately, sometimes feedback comes in the form of outcomes we do not want.

For example, when Cora Tsouflidou experienced her burnout, her body was telling her that things in her life were not working. Instead of ignoring what was happening, she needed to change her approach.

Cora Tsouflidou also listened to feedback to help create her restaurant's success. Her focus on making breakfasts to please her clients made her restaurant a hit. In fact, most of her menu items have a charming story behind them — how they were created to please a patron's favorite breakfast memory or flavor craving.

Being sensitive to her clients' feedback helped Cora Tsouflidou build her successful restaurant franchise.

Understanding Feedback

*"Before we determine whether feedback
is right or wrong, we first have to
understand it."*
— Douglas Stone & Sheila Heen [3]

Feedback can help you improve in many ways. Soliciting feedback is often the cheapest and easiest way to get better at a skill, create a superior product, or improve your ability to publicize your work.

No one can ever make you accept or implement feedback, but your really short change yourself if you do not try to understand the feedback that you are given. Most late bloomers take the time to appreciate comments or suggestions about their work.

However, there is always some feedback that is not helpful. Consider the painter Paul Cézanne, who's story we talked about in the first chapter. Paul Cézanne got a lot of negative feedback on his paintings. But he knew that the people offering the feedback did not understand what he was trying to do.

Feedback is not fact. It is someone's opinion. Figuring out what part of the feedback is actually of help is critical, then you can use the helpful bits of information to improve.

Summary

"Critics only make you stronger. You

have to look at what they are saying as
feedback. Sometimes the feedback helps,
and other times, it's just noise that can be
a distraction."

— Robert Kiyosaki

Late bloomers take advantage of useful feedback to reach their goals faster, but also learn how to ignore feedback that is simply discouragement or a form of distraction.

Chapter 12
Publicity

"Without promotion, something terrible happens... nothing!"

— P. T. Barnum

Painting only came into Grandma Moses' life when she was 78 years old.[1] But she received recognition for her paintings quite quickly in the United States.

Grandma Moses' tiny frame and plain spoken personality did not fit the traditional image of a successful painter. She started her working life as domestic help for a family, and married Thomas Salmon Moses who at the time was a farm hand.

Grandma Moses and her husband worked on several farms, until they could buy a farm of their own. Life could be very difficult. Five of Grandma Moses' children died as babies or were stillborn. Her heartache continued when her daughter Anna died as a young adult.

After retiring from her farming duties, Grandma Moses spent time embroidering pictures of farm life. But the work was painful because of the arthritis she had developed in her hands. Grandma Moses switched to painting, on the recommendation of her sister, and it was the perfect solution — allowing Grandma Moses a creative outlet without the pain. She started painting her memories of farm life. The results were charming paintings, filled with vibrant colors, that tugged on viewer's heart strings.

But how did Grandma Moses become an internationally renown painter, while quietly living on a farm in New York State? Well, she took some small steps toward publicity that helped develop her new painting career.

Small Steps Toward Publicity

"Whoever wants to reach a distant goal must take small steps."
— Saul Bellow

Late bloomers garner publicity using different approaches. At the start of her painting career Grandma Moses did two things to put her work in the public eye:

- First, she entered her paintings into the local county fair — she did not win any prizes for her paintings; interestingly, her fruit preserves did win some awards.

- Second, she had her paintings on display, and for sale, at the local drugstore. It was at the drugstore that a folk art collector, Louis Caldor, spotted her work.

Louis Caldor bought many of Grandma Moses' paintings. But his role went far beyond that of a collector. He was critical to Grandma Moses' painting career because he did the hard work of promoting Grandma Moses to art galleries. Initially, Louis Caldor faced resistance getting Grandma Moses' work displayed because some curators felt that Grandma Moses was too old to invest time and money promoting. However, Louis Caldor persisted and eventually got Grandma Moses' work displayed in New York's Museum of Modern Art, and her reputation and fan base grew from there.[2]

By putting her paintings into the public eye, Grandma Moses was discovered by a collector who was happy to put time and effort into promoting her work — and that made all the difference.

Big Steps Toward Publicity

Susan Boyle became an "overnight" success after she entered and sang on the talent show *Britain's Got Talent*. She was forty-eight years old. Susan Doyle's willingness to undertake a large step towards publicity made a huge difference in her career.

> *"There are enough people in the world who are going to write you off. You don't need to do that to yourself."*
>
> — Susan Boyle[3]

Before Susan took part in *Britain's Got Talent*, she had tried many other ways to improve her singing skills and promote her talent. In fact, Susan Boyle had a vocal coach, entered local talent contests, sang at her church, and took part in auditions.

However, it was Susan Boyle's appearances on *Britain's Got Talent* that got her the recognition she needed to share her talent with the world. Susan Boyle took a big step toward publicity to create the life she wanted.

When taking small steps to publicity does not get a late bloomer the results they are looking for, sometimes looking for bigger opportunities to display their work can be an effective strategy.

Publicity Outcomes

> *"Don't pay any attention to what they write about you. Just measure it in inches."*
> — Andy Warhol

Publicity can be tricky. Unfortunately, just because a person works hard, and promotes their work, it doesn't guarantee positive feedback. In fact, sometimes the feedback can sting or people may not even feel your work is worth displaying or commenting on at all. Consider one of the world's most influential painters, and for our purposes a *Messy Late Bloomer*, Paul Cézanne.

Paul Cézanne applied almost every year to get his paintings into the French "Salon" where a jury chose what art to display. Paul Cézanne was turned down pretty much every time. Getting approval of the "art establishment" didn't work for Cézanne — they didn't even want to display his work.

However, Paul Cézanne didn't give up, he still

managed to share some of his paintings with fellow artists and art dealers. He impressed many fellow artists, but more importantly he got the attention of art dealer Ambroise Vollard.

Vollard promoted Paul Cézanne's work and gave Paul his first independent art exhibition. This solo showing of Paul Cézanne's work would finally lead to some popular appreciation of his paintings.

Reformatting Work

> *"Stay committed to your decisions, but stay flexible in your approach."*
> — Tony Robbins

There are times when a late bloomer's talents can be difficult to share with a wider audience. Sometimes to become a late bloomer, it can be worthwhile to put your work into another format that the public can more easily appreciate. A good example is Norman Maclean.

Norman MacLean was a professor of English literature. He knew what good writing was, and he knew how to tell a story. His kids often told him to turn his stories into a book. But Norman Maclean did not find the time to do this until he retired.

While those around MacLean knew about his talents, it was with the publication of his book, *A River Run Through It and Other Stories*, three years after his retirement that Norman MacLean achieved broad acclaim.

Summary

> *"The woods would be quiet if no bird*
> *sang but the one that sang best."*
> — Henry van Dyke

Late-blooming success can be complicated. As people age, they are more likely to judge their accomplishments on their own terms; however, late bloomers often use broader acknowledgment and publicity to meet their goals. This is why successful late bloomers put their work in the public eye.

How late bloomers put their work into the public sphere can vary. While some late bloomers take small steps towards publicity, others will take much greater risks to get their work into public view. Moreover, some late bloomers may find it worthwhile to repackage their work into a format that is easier for the public to appreciate.

While no one can predict what the feedback will be when a piece of work is promoted, publicity is an important tool to promote late-blooming success.

Chapter 13
Following Through

"All great achievements require time."
— Maya Angelou

Estelle Getty got her big break as an actress at age 62, when she was cast as Sophia Petrillo on the hit show *The Golden Girls.*[1] What many people don't know is that Getty, who had raised two boys before she threw herself into her acting career, had actually spent years toiling in community theatre before her big break.

Following Through

While there are many different strategies to late blooming success, one of the most important is simply "stick-to-it-ness." In particular, following through on the many tasks and actions that a person knows is required to achieve their desired goal. There are many different ways to categorize the actions that require diligent follow through. One useful approach is to break down follow through into two categories:

1. Detail-orientated tasks; and,

2. Big-picture projects.

Let's look at each kind of follow-through topic separately.

1. Following Through on the Details

Following through on completing important details is a critical late-bloomer skill: whether it is making an important but unpleasant sales call, or giving a presentation that stretches a late bloomer's comfort zone. Unfortunately, there are many such uncomfortable, small steps that late bloomers need to complete in order to achieve their goals.

In the book, *Smarter, Better, Faster,* author Charles Duhigg, outlines how viewing these pesky, but necessary, tasks as part of achieving a greater goal, is extremely beneficial to over coming procrastination.[2]

Perhaps the greater perspective late bloomers have as they age improves their ability to frame following through on details as a meaningful activity.

Whatever strategy they choose to use, most successful late bloomers follow through on completing the details of their work.

2. Finishing Big-picture Projects

"Most people give up just when they're

*about to achieve success. They quit on
the one yard line. They give up at the
last minute of the game one foot from a
winning touchdown. "*

— Ross Perot

The end is often the hardest part. Whether it is the writer who can't bring themselves to send their finished manuscript to a publisher, or an artist who fails to display their work, following through on the final stages of a project is often the scariest part of an endeavor. However, it is also an important component of late-blooming success.

Late bloomers need to follow through on the difficult task of completing long-term projects, to make things happen. But perhaps late bloomers may have some advantages here. For example, for a young person the prospect of a failed project may be very frightening, and so procrastination may seem like a less painful alternative. On the other hand, most late bloomers have many failures under their belt, and have learned that failure is not such a terrible experience. This experience with failure, often makes a late bloomer more able to follow through with their work; as the downside of failure appears reduced and the prospect of success, still holds all the accompanying advantages.

Personal Benefits of Following Through

Following through with both the pesky details and the scary large tasks of a meaningful project takes a lot of energy and resources. One of the more common questions a late bloomer may ask themselves is: whether all that effort is worth it?

While late bloomers may find many of their skills

and abilities are heightened with age, people still usually have less endurance as they get older. And success, even with massive amounts of effort, is never guaranteed. However, the good news is that the longer we are fully engaged in a career or area of work, the healthier we are likely to be. So, a late bloomer can think of following through both as necessary to success, and as a method of improving well being. For example, in the "Longevity Project," a study that followed a group of smart kids throughout their lifetime, found that the people who lived the longest, and were the most contented, continued working long after others retired.[3]

> *"Those who stayed very involved in meaningful careers and worked the hardest, lived the longest."*
>
> — Howard S. Friedman[4]

Thus, it appears the hard work of following through on goal-related tasks, not only provides the benefit of increased odds of achievement, but also of increased personal well-being.

Summary

> *"Don't watch the clock; do what it does. Keep going."*
>
> — Sam Levenson

Following through with challenging work, can help late bloomers achieve success. Moreover, working for a long time in a meaningful career can be beneficial for a late bloomer's well-being.

Section Four

. . .

Getting Started: Now What?

Chapter 14
Experiment

*"All life is an experiment. The more
experiments you make the better."*
— Ralph Waldo Emerson

Elizabeth Layton was experiencing a severe depression
when she enrolled in an art class at the Ottawa University
at age 68.[1] This class changed her life.

Layton became a well-known, and celebrated artist
in the field of contour drawing. Her work integrated

self-portraits with reactions to social issues. Layton's work has been widely exhibited and is in the permanent collection of Smithsonian American Art Museum.[2]

Experimenting Towards a Late-blooming Journey

It is a common challenge for late bloomers to not know what area to focus their energies on. Being willing to experiment with new activities and endeavors is often a good way to kick start a late-blooming journey.

Elizabeth Layton's decision to take a university art class opened up a whole new world for her and started an exceptional journey of late-blooming success.

Late bloomers often approach finding an area of interest by following three simple steps.

1. Trying new things;

2. Using the results regardless; and

3. Repeating steps one and two, until they find something they want to pursue.

Let's look quickly at each of these steps.

1. Trying New Things

"A person who never made a mistake
never tried anything new."

— Albert Einstein

Remember late bloomer Cora Tsouflidou? She was searching for a new start, so she began by writing and drawing in her journal. However, her late-blooming adventure ended up taking her in an entirely different direction, she built a restaurant franchise that has over 130 locations.

To start your late-blooming adventure, there is no need to know exactly what direction your going; but you do need to at least start exploring the possibilities. Take a new course, try a new hobby, visit a new city. Expand and experiment with new activities and surroundings.

2. Use the Results, Regardless

If you find something you like on your first try, you're golden. But perhaps the more common situation for late bloomers, is that they try something new and it turns out they dislike it. But this information is absolutely useful.

In fact, Tony Robbins, a popular motivational and life coach, sometimes recommends that when a person is having a hard time finding their passion, they should describe what they would absolutely hate to do — then describe the opposite of this scenario, and a person has some pretty powerful clues as to their true calling.[3]

In this way, negative experiences provide a terrific amount of information about what to do next.

3. Repeat Steps 1 & 2 to Find a Compelling Activity

Ray Kroc worked a broad range of jobs including ambulance driver, DJ at a radio station, a paper cup salesman and milkshake machine salesman.[4]

Ray Kroc didn't stumble upon his true calling until he bought the rights to the McDonald's' restaurant system in his fifties. Kroc worked hard on building and franchising McDonald's and ended up creating the world's most successful restaurant franchise. Not surprisingly, he became very wealthy along the way.

Sometimes it takes many tries to find something that really resonates with a late bloomer. But whenever a person stumbles upon their true calling, great things are possible.

Summery

Starting a late-blooming journey can be an intimidating process. Consider approaching it the same way many other late bloomers have — by experimenting with many career options or projects. It often takes many tries for a late bloomer to find something they like. But each unsuccessful attempt can bring a person little closer to their true calling.

Chapter 15
Piecing it together

"To be yourself in a world that is constantly trying to make you something else is the greatest accomplishment."

— Ralph Waldo Emerson

When Harriet Doerr enrolled at Stanford University, after the death of her husband, she was 67 years old.[1] Doerr decided to study European History.

However, while at Stanford, Doerr also decided to start writing fiction. She eventually received the Stegner Fellowship in creative writing which provided her with educational writing workshops and encouragement to write.[2] Doerr began by writing short stories. But eventually moved on to novel writing. At 74, her first novel, *Stones for Ibarra,* was published. Doerr won a National Book award for this work.[3]

Doerr cobbled together different educational opportunities at Standford, with her rich life experiences, to create her personal late-blooming journey.

Piecing It Together

> *"Arrange whatever pieces*
> *come your way."*
>
> — Virginia Woolf

Creating late-blooming success can often feel like a hike uphill that doesn't have a clear path. This is because even once a late bloomer has found an activity that engages and inspires them, such as Harriet Doerr going back to school at age 67, there is still a long journey which needs to be pieced together to achieve late-blooming success.

While many late-blooming strategies can be easily extrapolated, this step is so individual that it is uniquely difficult to generalize. Perhaps, late bloomers must simply be both patient and persistent when piecing together their own path to success.

Late bloomers usually integrate their life experiences into their path, including the places they have lived, the people they have met, the books they have read, the jobs they have had, and their family experiences.

Somehow late bloomers must continue to sift, muddle, and explore the many options they have available until they find their path.

Remember Harriet Doerr? She moved from her new

studies in European History, to a fellowship in creative writing. Within her writing, she transitioned from short story writing to authoring a novel. And when she settled on a novel, it incorporated locations in Mexico where she had lived.

Summary

"There are no extra pieces in the universe. Everyone is here because he or she has a place to fill, and every piece must fit itself into the big jigsaw puzzle."

— Deepak Chopra

For late bloomers, piecing together their own unique path is a challenging and highly personal endeavor. It requires the late bloomer to integrate their own life experiences, current opportunities and personal preferences to create their own approach to late-blooming success.

Chapter 16
Dig In

"Real dreams take work. They take patience, and sometimes they require you to dig down very deep. Be sure you're willing to do that."

— Harvey Mackay

Giorgio Armani took a while to find his true calling. He spent a few years studying medicine at univeristy.[1] Next, Armani spent time working in the army. After his time in the military, Armani held several jobs including window dresser and clothing salesman.[2] Eventually, he found his way into designing clothes. By the time Armani founded his company "Armani" at age forty his was ready to dig in. He worked incredibly hard and was well rewarded. Giorgio Armani is now an iconic clothing designer and is thought to have a fortune of approximately 8.5 billion dollars.[3]

Dig In

When a late bloomer finds something thing they are interested in, they dig in. They spend a lot of time on their work.

Successful late bloomers, in particular, seem to dig in using more than one strategy. In the case of Giorgio Armani, he dug in using many strategies. He worked hard at mastering his designing skills and making incredible clothing collections, but he also pursued publicity for his clothing and company with a great deal of energy.

If you are unsure how to dig into your area of interest, consider going back and taking a look at chapters four through eight. These chapters look at how other late bloomers have dug into their work, the various approaches they took, and how it worked for them.

Digging in also often means, that as a late bloomer, you may be at this for a while. Remember, late bloomers often need to take their time to achieve in a specific area or endeavor.

Summary

> *"The secret of getting ahead is getting started."*
> — Mark Twain

Once a late bloomer has have figured out what work they would like to undertake in their late-blooming journey, they dig in.

Section Five

· · ·

Late
Bloomer
Lists

Chapter 17
Late-blooming
Entrepreneurs

"In business, experience is the big teacher."

— Matthew Stewart

There are many late-blooming entrepreneurs. Below is a list of just some of these people and a short summary of their real-life stories.

Entrepreneurs Who Were Late Bloomers

- **Ray Kroc**. Ray Kroc worked a broad range of jobs including DJ, paper cup salesman and mixer salesman.

Ray Kroc bought the rights to the McDonald's restaurant system in his fifties, and ended up creating the world's most successful restaurant franchise. Not surprisingly, he became very wealthy along the way.

- **Soichiro Honda.** Soichiro Honda founded Honda at forty years old. Prior to this, he had worked as a car mechanic, started his own car repair businesses and sold car parts. However, it wasn't until he founded Honda that his life's work of building motorcycles and cars began.

- **R. Buckminster Fuller.** R. Buckminster Fuller was expelled from college twice.[1] In his thirties, Fuller contemplated suicide, but found renewed strength by dedicating his life to inventing things that improved the life of others. By the time he was in his fifties, he became known internationally for things such as geodesic domes and his prolific writing.

- **Momofuke Ando.** In his youth, Momofuke Ando went bankrupt and to jail. However, he turned things around dramatically. Momofuke Ando invented and started to sell 'instant noodles' at age 48 and 'cup of noodles' at age 61. Momofuke Ando became a billionaire — and more importantly — provided affordable food to millions of people.

- **Giorgio Armani.** Giorgio Armani founded his fashion empire at 40 years of age. He needed to sell his car to do so. Before Armani started his company he had several jobs including selling menswear. Now in his eighties, he is estimated to be worth 8.5 billion dollars.[2]

- **John Pemberton.** John Pemberton created the carbonated version of Coca-Cola in his fifties, and figured out that it would sell better as a fountain drink than as a medicine (as he originally envisioned). Coca-Cola has gone on to be a worldwide soft drink brand.

- **Wally Blume.** Wally Blume started his ice cream company Denali Flavors at age 62. He created the very popular ice cream flavor "Moose Tracks."

- **Colonel Sanders.** Colonel Sanders was fired when he was a railway engineer, ended his career as a lawyer in a fistfight, and got canned as an insurance salesman. It wasn't until he was 65 years old that Colonel Sanders embarked on creating his famous KFC restaurant franchise, which became a huge success.

- **Margaret Rudkin.** Margaret Rudkin's son had asthma. His asthma grew worse if he ate food with artificial preservatives or flavors. Margaret Rudkin started baking wholesome bread that her son could eat comfortably. At age 40, she started making small batches of bread to sell. This was the beginning of the Pepperidge Farm company.

- **Cora Tsouflidou.** Cora Tsouflidou was a single mother and recovering from burnout when she founded Cora's a breakfast and lunch restaurant at 40 years old. There are now more than 130 Cora restaurants.[3]

- **Wally Amos.** Wally Amos started working in mail room at the William Morris Agency, and eventually became an agent. However, he got into financial trouble when he started his own agency. To deal with this challenge, he started making and selling "Famous Amos" gourmet cookies. They were a hit.

Chapter 18
Late-blooming
Athletes

"To enjoy the glow of good health, you must exercise."

— Gene Tunney

Contrary to conventional wisdom, there are many late-blooming athletes. Below is a list of just some of these people and a short summary of their real-life stories.

Athletes Who Were Late Bloomers

- **Robert Marchand**. Robert Marchand spent his adult years working a broad range of jobs including fireman, lumberjack, and shoe salesman.[1] He decided to focus on cycling at age 67, and began training seriously and participating in races. Robert Marchand is best known for setting the plus 100 year old cycling record at 102 years of age — by covering 16.7 miles in one hour. He also holds the record for the plus 100 year old cycling category by riding 62 miles (100 kilometers) in 4 hours, 17 minutes and 27 seconds.[2]

- **Diana Nyad.** Long-distance swimmer Diana Nyad decided to retire from swimming at age 29. But at age 60, she changed her mind and decided to return to swimming. Her goal was to be the first person to ever complete a swim from Cuba to Florida without using a shark cage — a goal she failed to meet in her twenties. It took her four years of practice and planning, as well as multiple attempts, but Diana Nyad successfully made the Cuba to Florida swim at 64 years old.

- **Oscar Swahn.** Oscar Swahn won his first Olympic gold medal at age 60, and became the oldest gold medalist at age 64 in the running deer, single shot events in 1912. He is also the oldest person to participate in the Olympic games, when he competed at 72 years old.

- **Tosca Reno.** Tosca Reno became overweight and out of shape in early adulthood. At forty, she decided to go back to the gym, eventually entering, and doing well in several body-building competitions. However, Tosca Reno did not stop there. She went on to become a best-selling author of the *Eat-Clean Diet* books, as well as a world-renown fitness coach.

- **Fauja Singh.** Fauja Singh started running at 84 years old to help him deal with the death of his wife and son. Fauja Singh ran his first marathon at age 89, and was the first 100 year old to complete a marathon.

- **Madonna Buder.** Madonna Buder is often referred to as the "Iron Nun," which is a reference to her participation in the physically demanding Ironman competitions and the fact that she is a nun at the Sisters for Christian Community convent. Madonna Buder started training at 48 years old. She completed her first triathlon at 52 years old, and her first Ironman at 55.[3] In 2012, she became the oldest woman to complete a demanding Ironman race at 82 years old.

- **Ray Moon.** Ray Moon became a body builder in his seventies, and has won several Australian amateur competitions. He was not particularly fit before he started. In fact, Moon had experienced many health setbacks including a heart attack before he started weight training. Now, he holds the Guinness World Record as the world's oldest body builder.[4]

- **Olga Kotelko.** Olga Kotelko was a teacher, and a single parent for most of her life. After she retired at 65 years old, she took up softball. At age 77, she switched to track and field. Between ages 77 and 95, Olga earned 37 world track and field records in her age category including the 100 meter, 200 meter, and long jump events.[5]

- **Francis Chichester.** Francis Chichester sailed around the world at 65 years old. It took him over nine months to do so — a record at that time.[6] Notably, when Chichester was 57 years old, he was diagnosed with terminal lung cancer. He went on a vegetarian diet, and recovered from the illness. Prior to his athletic career, Chichester had many jobs including miner, salesman and map-publisher.[7]

Chapter 19
Late-blooming
Visual Artists

*"I am always doing that which
I cannot do, in order that I may learn
how to do it."*

— Pablo Picasso

There are many late-blooming visual artists. Below is a list of just some of these people and a short summary of their real-life stories.

Visual Artists Who Were Late Bloomers

- **Mary Delany.** Mary Delany was twice widowed.

After the death of her second husband, she focused on making intricate paper cutouts of plants and flowers to help her cope with the loss. These cutouts were so exquisite that they are now part of the British Museum's collection.[1] Mrs. Delany created over 1,700 of these pieces of art, working until age 88.[2]

- **Paul Cézanne.** Paul Cézanne painted his entire adult life. He was largely considered a failed painter in his forties. However, he persisted and his reputation and painting skills took off in his fifties and sixties.

- **Auguste Rodin.** Auguste Rodin worked as a craftsman for other artists and sculptors for the first twenty years of his career; after which, he became one of the most celebrated sculptors of all time.

- **Louise Nevelson.** Louise Nevelson spent a long time as a broke, struggling artist. Her career took off in her fifties, but stalled after a difficult deal with a gallery. However, she continued to work and from her late sixties onward she created some of her best work, and most financially successful art.

- **Noah Purifoy.** Noah Purifoy earned teaching and social work degrees before he embarked into the world of art. He is best known for his found-art sculpture displayed in the desert, in Joshua Tree, California. Noah did not even begin his work in Joshua Tree, until he moved there when he was 72 years old.

- **Grandma Moses.** Grandma Moses worked on a farm most of her life. She only started painting in her late seventies. However, she enjoyed over twenty years of painting success and became folk art sensation with her work on display, and for sale, worldwide.

Grandma Moses painted until her death at 101 years old.

- **Bill Traylor.** Bill Traylor was broke and homeless at 85 years old. To pass the time, he started drawing and displaying his work on the streets of Montgomery, Alabama. Bill created many works of art, which are now widely celebrated.

- **Louise Bourgeois.** Louise Bourgeois worked as an artist most of her life. However, her artistic success came slowly. In fact, Louise's most memorable and financially successful sculptures were created after she was 80 years old. In particular, her giant sculpture of a spider titled "Maman," was first displayed when Louise Bourgeois was 89 years old. The sculpture has sold for millions of dollars and been exhibited around the world.[3]

- **William Edmondson.** Edmondson worked as a laborer and a janitor most of his life. After the hospital that he worked at as a janitor closed, Edmondson turned to sculpture. By that time he was in his sixties. He received a one-man show at the Museum of Modern Art in New York City. His work is still noted and displayed.

- **Irving Dominick.** Irving Dominick spent his life working with sheet metal making practical things such as duct work and gutters. After he retired, he used his skills to make works of art. Some of his sculpture can now be seen at the Smithsonian American Art Museum.

- **Elizabeth Layton.** Elizabeth Layton was experiencing a severe depression when she enrolled in an art class at Ottawa University at age 68. This class changed her life. She became a well-known, and celebrated artist in the field of contour drawing. Her work integrated self-portraits with reactions to social issues. Her work has been widely exhibited and is in the permanent collection of Smithsonian American Art Museum.

Chapter 20
Late-blooming
Performers

*"I look to the future because that's where
I'm going to spend the rest of my life."*

— George Burns

There are many late-blooming performers. Below is a list of just some of these people and a short summary of their real-life stories.

Performers Who Were Late Bloomers

- **Joy Behar.** Joy Behar decided to switch careers in her early forties. She went from being a teacher to an aspiring comedian and performer. She started her new career as a receptionist at NBC. She later became a lauded comedian, co-host of the popular daytime show *The View*, and acted in several movies.

- **Clara Peller.** Clara Peller was a manicurist for over 35 years. She was "discovered" in her eighties when she worked as manicurist on a TV set.[1] Clara starred in many commercials. She is best known for her role in a Wendy's commercial where she asks: "Where's the beef?"

- **Mae Laborde.** Mae Laborde worked as a sales clerk and, later, a bookkeeper.[2] She was 93 years old when she started her acting career. She is known for playing the part of Gladis in *It's Always Sunny in Philadelphia*.

- **Estelle Getty.** Estelle Getty waited to dive into her acting career until she had raised her two boys. She is best known as Sophia Petrillio on the comedy series the *Golden Girls*. It was a role Estelle landed when she was 62 years old.

- **John Mahoney.** John Mahoney was an editor of a medical journal before he turned to acting. He was 45 when he got his first movie role. He is best known for his work on the hit TV sitcom *Fraiser*, playing Martin Crane — a role he landed when he was 53 years old.

- **Phyllis Diller.** Phyllis Diller had six children with her first husband before starting her career in comedy and television.[3] She appeared regularly on TV shows such as the *Tonight Show*, and also did voice work for animated shows such as *Family Guy*.

- **Susan Boyle.** Susan Boyle sang at her church from an early age, but she didn't get her big break until she was 48 years old — when she entered and sang on the talent show *Britain's Got Talent*. Susan has now sold millions of records.

- **Sharon Jones.** Sharon Jones always loved to sing but worked as a corrections officer and at a bank before her music career took off in her forties. Sharon Jones & The Dap-Kings have released numerous records.

- **Kathryn Joosten**. Kathryn Joosten began her career as a nurse. She started participating in community theatre at 42 years old.[4] At age 56, Kathryn moved to Hollywood. Kathryn landed roles in many different sitcoms, but is best known for her role in *Desperate Housewives* as Karen McCluskey for which she won two Emmys.

- **Julia Child.** Julia Child really hit her stride in her fifties when she began hosting a cooking show. Sharing her sense of humor, cooking skills, and impressive presentation skills on her TV show helped make her a great late bloomer.

Chapter 2I
Late-blooming
Writers

"Your creative potential at any age is built upon your life experience, but not limited to it."

— Gene Cohen

There are many late-blooming writers. Below is a list of just some of these people and a short summary of their real-life stories.

Writers Who Were Late Bloomers

- **Donald Ray Pollock.** Donald Ray Pollock worked for 32 years in a paper mill.[1] At 50 years old, he quit his job, and enrolled in a university English program. His his first book, *Knockemstiff*, was published when Pollock was 54 years old.[2]

- **Harry Bernstein**. Harry Bernstein was devastated after the death of his wife. To help him cope, the 93 year old wrote *The Invisible Wall* which is a memoir about his childhood. The book became a huge success. It was published when Mr. Bernstein was 96 years old.

- **Peter Roget.** Peter Roget retired from his scientific and medical career at 69 years old. He decided that in retirement he would turn his preoccupation with making lists of words into a useful book. After four years of solid work, the *Roget's Thesaurus* was published. Peter Roget was 73 years old. *Roget's Thesaurus* has sold over 32 million copies.[3]

- **Laura Ingalls Wilder.** Laura Ingalls Wilder wrote her *Little House* series of books in her sixties. The first *Little House* book was published when Wilder was 65 years old. The books were also made into the popular TV series *Little House on the Prairie* starring Melissa Gilbert and Michael Landon.

- **Elizabeth Jolly.** Elizabeth Jolly was trained as a nurse, but always had an interest in writing. However, her first book was not published until she was 53 years old. She continued writing and ended up publishing fourteen more books. Jolly won many awards for writing and became a professor of creative writing at 75 years old.

- **Frank McCourt.** Frank McCourt wrote his award-winning book *Angela's Ashes* after retiring from his high school teaching career. The book has sold millions of copies.

- **Raymond Chandler.** Raymond Chandler worked for an oil company, but decided to become a writer in his forties after he lost his job. He penned many successful books including *The Big Sleep* and *Farewell, My Lovely*.

- **Wallace Stevens.** Wallace Stevens spent most of his working life as an insurance executive. However, he also wrote poetry. His poetry matured and evolved over time, and his best work was done later in life. Wallace Stevens won the Pulitzer Prize at 75 years old.

- **Norman Maclean.** Norman MacLean wrote the book *A River Run Through It and Other Stories*, three years after his retirement from his career as a university professor. It was his first book of fiction, and his most acclaimed work.

- **Robert Frost.** Robert Frost was a poet for most of his life. But he worked in various jobs, such as a farmer and a teacher, to make ends meet. It was only in his fifties that his reputation as a poet was truly established. Frost's work grew more impressive over time. He won four Pulitzer Prizes — at ages 50, 57, 63, and 69.[4]

- **Harriet Doerr** had her first book, *Stones for Ibarra*, published when she as 73 years old.[5] She won an American Book Award for the work. She followed that with a second book, *Consider This, Señora*, published when she was 83 years old.

Chapter 22
Late-blooming
Activists & Politicians

"Life is not accumulation, it is about contribution."

— Stephen Covey

There are many late-blooming activists and politicians. Below is a list of just some of these people and a short summary of their real-life stories.

Politicians and Activists Who Were Late Bloomers

- **Nelson Mandela**. Nelson Mandela became the President of the Republic of South Africa at 75 years of age. Prior to being elected, he was a political prisoner for 27 years.[1] Mandela won the Nobel Peace Prize for negotiating the end of apartheid in South Africa.

- **Ronald Regan.** Ronald Regan became President of the United States at 69 years old. He was initially a sportscaster and actor. He later became active in politics, first becoming the Governor of California, and then the President of the US. When he stepped down as President of the United States at 77 years old, he had a very high approval rating.

- **Marjorie Stoneman Douglas.** Marjorie Stoneman Douglas became an environmental crusader at 79 years old. Her ability to connect with people though her speeches and conversations helped conserve the the Florida Everglades and limit development on this environmentally sensitive area. She was awarded the Presidential Medal of Freedom for her work.

- **Bernie Sanders.** Bernie Sanders learned how to get elected the hard way — by losing his first four elections. But Bernie didn't give up. He finally got elected as Mayor of Burlington, Vermont in 1981, and was the Mayor for eight years. Sanders then went on to become an independent Member of Congress for 16 years, and later a senator.

- **Edward Ricardo (E.R.) Braithwaite.** E.R. Braithwaite couldn't find a job in his chosen field of engineering so he ended up becoming a teacher in a poor school in London, England. He wrote a book about his experiences there, titled *To Sir with Love*. The book was published when he was 47 years old.[2] The book opened the door for him to work as a consultant and diplomat. Braithwaite became a consultant for United Nations Educational, Scientific and Cultural Organization; as well as ambassador to Venezuela (on behalf of Guyana); and an academic.[3]

- **Mother Teresa.** Mother Teresa left home at age 18 to join a convent and become a nun. She spent twenty years as part of the convent and as a teacher. After this time, she felt the call to serve the poorest of the poor, and received permission to leave the convent.[4] She founded her Missionaries of Charity at forty years old.[5] Mother spent the rest of her life serving the poorest people in India. At age 69, she was awarded the Nobel Peace Prize.[6]

Section Six

...

The Rest

Conclusion

"As long as we are persistent in our pursuit of our deepest destiny, we will continue to grow. We cannot choose the day or time when we will fully bloom. It happens in its own time."

— Denis Waitley

Late bloomers reach their late-in-life success in different ways. However, each person's story is uniquely filled with hope, obstacles, persistence and fulfillment.

I hope this book has opened your eyes to some of the great possibilities that the second half of life may hold, as well as many of the strategies that late bloomers use to help them continue on their unique path to success.

Let your own late-blooming adventure begin...

End Notes

Chapter 1: Messy Late Bloomers

1. Josh Ozersky, *Colonel Sanders and the American Dream* (Austin: University of Texas Press, 2012), 7.

2. http://www.kfc.com/about.

3. Josh Ozersky, *Colonel Sanders and the American Dream.*

4. Francine Lafontaine and Kathryn Shaw, "Serial Entrepreneurship: Learning by Doing?" *NBER Working Paper No. 20312*, July 2014.

5. http://www.vanityfair.com/unchanged/2012/02/qatar-buys-cezanne-card-players-201202.

6. David W.Galenson, *Old masters and young geniuses the two life cycles of artistic creativity* (Princeton, N.J. : Princeton University Press, 2006).

Chapter 2: Bad News Late Bloomers

1. Madeleine Albright and Bill Woodward, *Madam Secretary* (New York: Mirmax Books, 2003).

2. https://en.wikipedia.org/wiki/Madeleine_Albright.

3. Albright and Woodward, *Madam Secretary.*

4. https://en.wikipedia.org/wiki/Margaret_Rudkin.

5. Nader Badshah, "The world's oldest runner, Fauja Singh, on life since his retirement" *The Guardian,* accessed at http://www.theguardian.com/lifeandstyle/the-running-blog/2013/

oct/11/ fauja-singh-worlds-oldest-runner-102.

6. https://en.wikipedia.org/wiki/Fauja_Singh.

7. Richard G. Tedeschi and Lawrence G. Calhoun, "Beyond the Concept of Recovery: Growth and the Experience of Loss," *Death Studies*, 32: 27–39, 2008.

8. Richard G. Tedeschi, Lawrence G. Calhoun and Arnie Cann, "Evaluating Resource Gain: Understanding and Misunderstanding Posttraumatic Growth" *Applied Psychology: An International Review*, 2007, 56 (3), 396–406.

Chapter 3: New Stage Late Bloomers

1. http://www.thestar.com/entertainment/2009/07/19/angelas_ashes_author_frank_mccourt_dies_at_78.html.

2. https://en.wikipedia.org/wiki/Raymond_Chandler.

3. https://en.wikipedia.org/wiki/Bill_Traylor.

4. Ibid.

5. http://www.penguin.co.uk/books/rogets-thesaurus-of-english-words-and-phrases/9780141004426/.

Chapter 4: The Experience Advantage

1. Tanya Lee Stone, *Laura Ingalls Wilder* (New York, NY: DK Publishing, 2009)

2. Ibid.

3. http://www.ala.org/alsc/awardsgrants/bookmedia/newberymedal/newberyhonors/newberymedal#30s

4. http://www.krannert.purdue.edu/konline/fall2009/tracks.asp

5. Ibid.

6.   Ibid.

7.   Deborah, K Ray, *Hokusai: The Man Who Painted a Mountain,* (New York, Farrar, Straus and Giroux, 2001).

8.   Katsushika quote in *The Crown of Life: Artistic Creativity in Old Age*, by Hugo Munsterberg, (San Diego: Harcourt Brace Jovanovich Publishers, 1983) p. 55.

9.   https://en.wikipedia.org/wiki/Hokusai.

Chapter 5: The Perspective Advantage

1.   Quote of R. Buckminster Fuller in Jackie Craven's article "R. Buckminster Fuller," *Architect Philosopher*, http://architecture. about.com/od/greatarchitects/p/fuller.htm.

2.   https://en.wikipedia.org/wiki/Buckminster_Fuller.

3.   https://en.wikipedia.org/wiki/John_Mahoney

4.   http://www.imdb.com/name/nm0001498/bio?ref_=nm_ov_bio_sm.

5.   https://en.wikipedia.org/wiki/Louise_Bourgeois.

6.   Quote of Harry Bernstein in "Successful at 96, Writer Has More to Say" by Motoko Rich, *The New York Times Online* at http://www.nytimes.com/2007/04/07/books/07bern. html?n=Top/ Reference/Times%20Topics/People/R/Rich,%20 Motoko&_r=0&pagewanted=all.

Chapter 6: Mindful Advantage

1.   Igor Grossmann1, Jinkyung Na, Michael E.W. Varnum et al. "A Route to Well-being: Intelligence vs. Wise Reasoning" The *Journal of Experimental Psychology: General*, 2013 August; 142(3): 944–953.

2.   https://www.psychologytoday.com/basics/wisdom.

3. Susan Turk Charles and Laura L. Carstensen, "Unpleasant Situations Elicit Different Emotional Responses in Younger and Older Adults" *Psychology and Aging,* 2008 September ; 23(3): 495–504.

4. Ibid.

5. M. Mather & A. Ponzio, "Emotion and Aging." in L. Barrett & M. Lewis *et al. Handbook of Emotions.*

6. Ibid.

Chapter 7: Internal Motivation

1. Arnold B Glimcher, *Louise Nevelson* (New York: EP Dutton & Co, 1976).

2. Christian Stamov-Roßnagel, and Guido Hertel, "Older workers' motivation: against the myth of general decline" *Management Decision*, 2010, Vol. 48, Iss 6, 894 - 906.

Chapter 8: Master a Skill

1. Janina Boyke et al.,"Training-induced brain structure changes in the elderly" *The Journal of Neuroscience,* July 9, 2008, Vol.28(28), pp.7031-5.

2. Stanley J. Colcombe et al., "Aerobic Exercise Training Increases Brain Volume in Aging Humans" *The Journal's of Gerontology Series A: Biological Sciences and Medical Sciences*, 2006, Vol. 61(11), pp.1166-1170.

3. Kirk Erickson et al., "Exercise training increases size of hippocampus and improves memory" *Proceedings of the National Academy of Sciences of the United States of America,* 15 February 2011, Vol.108(7), pp.3017-3022.

4. Joe Verghese, Richard B. Lipton *et al.* "Leisure Activities and the Risk of Dementia in the Elderly" *New England Journal of*

Medicine 2003; 348:2508-2516

5. Laura A. Whitlock et. al., "Individual differences in response to cognitive training: Using a multi-modal, attentionally demanding game-based intervention for older adults" *Computers in Human Behavior,* 2012, Vol. 28(4), pp.1091-1096.

6. http://www.cnn.com/2013/09/02/world/americas/diana-nyad-cuba-florida-swim/

7. Ibid.

8. Ericsson, K. Anders and Neil Charness, "Expert performance: its structure and acquisition" *The American Psychologist,* August, 1994, Vol. 49(8), pp.725-747, p. 738.

9. Ibid.

10. Ralf T. Kampe, *Maintaining excellence: Cognitive-motor performance in pianists differing in age and skill level* (Berlin: Edition Sigma, 1994).

11. David Pink, *Drive: The surprising truth about what motivates us* (New York: Riverhead Books, 2009), p. 124.

12. David Shenk, *The genius in all of us: A new science of genes, talent, and intelligence* (New York : Doubleday 2010).

13. Ibid.

14. K. Anders Ericsson, Ralf Th. Krampe, and Clemens Tesch-Romer, "The Role of Deliberate Practice in the Acquisition of Expert Performance" *Psychological Review* (1993) Vol. 100. No. 3, 363-406.

15. Carol Dweck, *Mindset: The new psychology of success* (New York: Random House 2006).

16. Ibid.

Chapter 9: Unique Skill Set

1. Scott Adams, *How to fail at almost everything and still win big: Kind of the story of my life* (New York: Portfolio/Penguin, 2013) p. 98.

2. Bob Spitz, *Dearie: the remarkable life of Julia Child* (New York: Knopf, 2012).

3. https://en.wikipedia.org/wiki/Momofuku_Ando.

4. Ibid.

5. Julia Cameron, *The artist's way: a spiritual path to higher creativity* (Los Angeles: Jeremy P. Tarcher/Putnam, 2002).

6. https://en.wikipedia.org/wiki/Clara_Peller.

7. Ibid.

Chapter 10: Key Relationships

1. Malcolm Gladwell, *Outliers: the story of success* (New York: Little Brown, 2008).

2. http://www.npr.org/2014/05/28/316707321/fresh-air-remembers-poet-and-memoirist-maya-angelou.

3. Richard Wiseman, *The luck factor : changing your luck, changing your life: the four essential principles* (New York: Miramax, 2003).

4. https://www.guggenheim.org/the-frank-lloyd-wright-building.

5. https://en.wikipedia.org/wiki/Manoel_de_Oliveira.

6. Ibid.

7. Ibid.

8. https://en.wikipedia.org/wiki/Marjory_Stoneman_Douglas.

9. Ibid.

10. Ibid.

Chapter 11: Getting and Using Feedback

1. Cora Tsouflidou, translation by Dawn M. Cornelio, *Breakfast with Cora* (Toronto: McArthur & Co., 2010) p. 56.

2. http://www.chezcora.com/en/about-cora.

3. Douglas Stone & Sheila Heen, *Thanks for the Feedback: The Science and Art of Receiving Feedback Well* (New York: Viking, 2014) p. 46.

Chapter 12: Publicity

1. https://en.wikipedia.org/wiki/Grandma_Moses.

2. Ibid.

3. Susan Boyle, *The woman I was born to be: my story* (New York: Atria Books, 2010).

Chapter 13: Following Through

1. https://en.wikipedia.org/wiki/Estelle_Getty

2. Charles Duhigg, *Smarter, faster, better: the secrets of being productive in life and business* (New York, NY: Random House, 2016).

3. Howard Friedman response to question in article by Amy Novotney, "The real secrets to a longer life. Howard S. Friedman says that eating vegetables and going to the gym are not as important to our long-term health as having a rich, productive life" *American Psychological Association*, December 2011, Vol 42, No 11, p. 36.

4. Amy Novotney, "The real secrets to a longer life. Howard

S. Friedman says that eating vegetables and going to the gym are not as important to our long-term health as having a rich, productive life" *American Psychological Association*, December 2011, Vol 42, No 11, p. 36.

Chapter 14: Experiment

1. https://en.wikipedia.org/wiki/Elizabeth_Layton.

2. Ibid.

3. Anthony Robbins, *Unleash the Power Within: Personal Coaching from Anthony Robbins That Will Transform Your Life!* (Simon & Schuster Audio/Nightingale-Conant, 1999).

4. http://www.biography.com/people/ray-kroc-9369349#early-life.

Chapter 15: Piecing It Together

1. https://en.wikipedia.org/wiki/Harriet_Doerr.

2. Ibid.

3. Ibid.

Chapter 16: Dig In

1. https://en.wikipedia.org/wiki/Giorgio_Armani.

2. Ibid.

3. Ibid.

Chapter 17: Late-blooming Entrepreneurs

1. https://en.wikipedia.org/wiki/Buckminster_Fuller.

2. https://en.wikipedia.org/wiki/Giorgio_Armani.

3. http://www.chezcora.com/en/about-cora.

Chapter 18: Late-Blooming Athletes

1. http://espn.go.com/olympics/cycling/story/_/id/10383489/102-year-old-french-cyclist-robert-marchand-sets-world-record.

2. https://de.wikipedia.org/wiki/Robert_Marchand translated from French to English by Bing Translation.

3. https://en.wikipedia.org/wiki/Madonna_Buder.

4. http://www.laterbloomer.com/late-blooming-athletes/.

5. http://www.olgakotelko.com/biography/.

6. http://www.telegraph.co.uk/sport/othersports/sailing/2355079/Chichester-took-a-break-and-he-needed-one.html.

7. Editors of Encyclopædia Britannica, "Sir Francis Chichester, British Adventurer" *Encyclopædia Britannica Online*, https://www.britannica.com/biography/Francis-Chichester.

Chapter 19: Late-blooming Visual Artists

1. http://www.britishmuseum.org/explore/highlights/highlight_objects/pd/m/mary_delany,_passiflora_laurif.aspx.

2. https://en.wikipedia.org/wiki/Mary_Delany.

3. https://en.wikipedia.org/wiki/Maman_(sculpture).

Chapter 20: Late-blooming Performers

1. https://en.wikipedia.org/wiki/Clara_Peller.

2. http://www.kazantoday.com/WeeklyArticles/mae-laborde.html.

3. https://en.wikipedia.org/wiki/Phyllis_Diller.

4. https://en.wikipedia.org/wiki/Kathryn_Joosten

Chapter 21: Late-blooming Writers

1. http://donaldraypollock.net/bio-4.

2. https://en.wikipedia.org/wiki/Donald_Ray_Pollock.

3. https://www.penguin.com.au/products/9780140515039/roget-s-thesaurus-english-words-phrases.

4. https://en.wikipedia.org/wiki/Robert_Frost.

5. http://www.nytimes.com/2002/11/27/arts/harriet-doerr-is-dead-at-92-writer-of-searing-sparse-prose.html?_r=0.

Chapter 22: Late-blooming Activists & Politicians

1. https://www.nelsonmandela.org/content/page/timeline.

2. https://en.wikipedia.org/wiki/E._R._Braithwaite.

3. Ibid.

4. http://www.vatican.va/news_services/liturgy/saints/ns_lit_doc_20031019_madre-teresa_en.html

5. Ibid.

6. Ibid.

Image Sources

Introduction

- Butterfly, public domain image from www.pixabay.com.

Chapter 1: Messy Late Bloomers

- Splat, public domain image from www.pixabay.com.

- Chart for *Messy Late Bloomers* by JMO.

- Paul Cézanne, self-portrait, circa 1895, public domain image from https://en.wikipedia.org/wiki/Paul_Cézanne#/media/File:Paul_Cézanne_151.jpg.

- *The Card Players*, by Paul Cézanne, circa 1892–95, public domain image from https://upload.wikimedia.org/wikipedia/commons/d/d4/Paul_Cézanne%2C_1892-95%2C_Les_joueurs_de_carte_%28The_Card_Players%29%2C_60_x_73_cm%2C_oil_on_canvas%2C_Courtauld_Institute_of_Art%2C_London.jpg.

Chapter 2: Bad News Late Bloomers

- Sad cartoon drawing, public domain image from www.pixabay.com.

- Chart for *Bad News Late Bloomers* by JMO.

- Question marks, public domain image from www.pixabay.com.

Chapter 3: New Stage Late Bloomers

- New start drawing, public domain image from www.pixabay.com

- Chart for New Stage Late Bloomers by JMO.

- Photo of Peter Mark Roget (c. 1865) taken by Ernest Edwards,

1837-1903, public domain image from https://upload.wikimedia.org/wikipedia/commons/8/8c/Peter_Mark_Roget.jpg.

Chapter 4: The Experience Advantage

- Hard knocks image by JMO.
- *Katsushika Hokusai Self-portrait* (1839), public domain image from https://en.wikipedia.org/wiki/Hokusai#/media/File:Hokusai_portrait.png.
- *Thirty-six Views of Mount Fuji, no. 27.* (Umezawa in Sagami Province), public domain image from https://en.wikipedia.org/wiki/Thirty-six_Views_of_Mount_Fuji#/media/File:Umegawa_in_Sagami_province.jpg.

Chapter 5: The Perspective Advantage

- Globe, public domain image from www.pixabay.com.

Chapter 6: The Mindful Advantage

- Yoga pose, public domain image from www.pixabay.com.

Chapter 7: Internal Motivation

- Why post-it, public domain image from www.pixabay.com
- Photo of Rodin, date unknowing, public domain image from https://upload.wikimedia.org/wikipedia/commons/7/72/Rodin-cropped.png.
- *The Thinker* (1879–1889), sculpture by Rodin, public domain image from https://upload.wikimedia.org/wikipedia/commons/5/56/The_Thinker%2C_Rodin.jpg.

Chapter 8: Master a Skill

- Skill, public domain image from www.pixabay.com.
- Heart beat drawing, public domain image from www.pixabay.com.

Chapter 9: Unique Skill Set

- Snowflake, public domain image from www.pixabay.com.
- Hat, public domain image from www.pixabay.com.

Chapter 10: Key Relationships

- Handshake, public domain image from www.pixabay.com.

Chapter 11: Getting & Using Feedback

- Stars, public domain image from www.pixabay.com.

Chapter 12: Publicity

- Megaphone, public domain image from www.pixabay.com.
- Footsteps, public domain image from www.pixabay.com.

Chapter 13: Following Through

- Turtle, public domain image from www.pixabay.com.

Chapter 14: Experiment

- Scientist, public domain image from www.pixabay.com.

Chapter 15: Piecing it Together

- Puzzle pieces, public domain image from www.pixabay.com.

Chapter 16: Digging In

- Shovel, public domain image from www.pixabay.com.

Chapter 17: Late-blooming Entrepreneurs

- On sale sign, public domain image from www.pixabay.com.

Chapter 18: Late-blooming Athletes

- Sneakers, public domain image from www.pixabay.com.

Chapter 19: Late-blooming Visual Artist

- Portrait, public domain image from www.pixabay.com

Chapter 20: Late-blooming Performers

- Masks, public domain image from www.pixabay.com.

Chapter 21: Late-blooming Writers

- Pen, public domain image from www.pixabay.com.

Chapter 22: Late-blooming Politicians & Activists

- Podium, public domain image from www.pixabay.com.

About the Author
J.M. Orend

*"There are two ways of spreading light:
to be the candle or the mirror that
reflects it."*
— Edith Wharton

I am grateful to have had the opportunity to research the lives of so many late bloomers. Not only has it resulted in this book, but it has transformed how I approach my own work.

It is my hope that by writing and reflecting on the success people have achieved later in life, readers will find their own path to becoming a late bloomer a little brighter.

I appreciate the time you have spent reading *Successful Late Bloomers*. If you would like to know more about my work and other books, please check out www.jmorend.com.

Made in the USA
Lexington, KY
09 July 2018